Cicero *Pro Cluentio*

The following titles are available from Bloomsbury for the OCR specifications in Latin and Greek for examinations from June 2021 to June 2023

Catullus: A Selection of Poems, with introduction, commentary notes and vocabulary by John Godwin

Cicero *Pro Cluentio*: A Selection, with introduction, commentary notes and vocabulary by Matthew Barr

Livy *History of Rome* I: A Selection, with introduction, commentary notes and vocabulary by John Storey

Ovid *Heroides*: A Selection, with introduction, commentary notes and vocabulary by Christina Tsaknaki

Tacitus *Annals* IV: A Selection, with introduction, commentary notes and vocabulary by Robert Cromarty

Virgil *Aeneid* XII: A Selection, with introduction, commentary notes and vocabulary by James Burbidge

OCR Anthology for Classical Greek AS and A Level, covering the prescribed texts by Aristophanes, Homer, Plato, Plutarch, Sophocles and Thucydides, with introduction, commentary notes and vocabulary by Simon Allcock, Sam Baddeley, John Claughton, Alastair Harden, Sarah Harden, Carl Hope and Jo Lashley

Supplementary resources for these volumes can be found at www.bloomsbury.com/OCR-editions-2021-2023
Please type the URL into your web browser and follow the instructions to access the Companion Website. If you experience any problems, please contact Bloomsbury at academicwebsite@bloomsbury.com

Cicero *Pro Cluentio*: A Selection

Taken from *Murder at Larinum*, Chapters 1–7, 10–11, 27–32, 35–37

With introduction, commentary notes and vocabulary by Matthew Barr

BLOOMSBURY ACADEMIC
LONDON • NEW YORK • OXFORD • NEW DELHI • SYDNEY

BLOOMSBURY ACADEMIC
Bloomsbury Publishing Plc
50 Bedford Square, London, WC1B 3DP, UK
1385 Broadway, New York, NY 10018, USA

BLOOMSBURY, BLOOMSBURY ACADEMIC and the Diana logo
are trademarks of Bloomsbury Publishing Plc

First published in Great Britain 2020

Cover design: Terry Woodley
Cover image © PjrTravel / Alamy Stock Photo

A catalogue record for this book is available from the British Library.

A catalog record for this book is available from the Library of Congress.

ISBN: PB: 978-1-3500-6034-0
ePDF: 978-1-3500-6036-4
eBook: 978-1-3500-6035-7

Typeset by RefineCatch Limited, Bungay, Suffolk
Printed and bound in India

Contents

The teaching content of this resource is endorsed by OCR for use with specification AS Level Latin (H043) and specification A Level Latin (H443). In order to gain OCR endorsement, this resource has been reviewed against OCR's endorsement criteria.

This resource was designed using the most up to date information from the specification. Specifications are updated over time which means there may be contradictions between the resource and the specification, therefore please use the information on the latest specification and Sample Assessment Materials at all times when ensuring students are fully prepared for their assessments.

Any references to assessment and/or assessment preparation are the publisher's interpretation of the specification requirements and are not endorsed by OCR. OCR recommends that teachers consider using a range of teaching and learning resources in preparing learners for assessment, based on their own professional judgement for their students' needs. OCR has not paid for the production of this resource, nor does OCR receive any royalties from its sale. For more information about the endorsement process, please visit the OCR website, www.ocr.org.uk.

Preface

The text and notes found in this volume are designed to guide any student who has mastered Latin up to GCSE level and wishes to read Cicero's text of *Pro Cluentio* in the original.

The edition is, however, particularly designed to support students who are reading Cicero's text in preparation for OCR's AS and A Level Latin examination June 2021–June 2023. (Please note this edition uses AS to refer indiscriminately to AS and the first year of A Level, i.e. Group 1.)

The *Pro Cluentio* is an excellent example of Cicero's oratorical powers; by this point in his career, Cicero has gained a significant reputation due to his previous lawcourt speeches. He presents a concise, logical argument whilst keeping his intended audience engaged in the narrative of the case. At times, this speech reads like some unbelievable novel, with characters so vivid (and so melodramatic) that we, like the ancient audience, feel swept away by Cicero's narrative. The *Pro Cluentio* also gives us an insight into life in a *municipium* (a country town) at a rather turbulent time in the history of the Roman Republic; clearly war has had an effect on the people of the small town of Larinum and it provides an interesting look at how events affected the rest of Italy rather than just the city of Rome. However, perhaps the most fascinating part of this speech is the narrative concerning Oppianicus the Elder and Sassia, presenting the two as the ultimate antagonists in an ancient killing spree. A tale of gruesome murders, adultery, theft and revenge, the *Pro Cluentio* certainly forms one of Cicero's more entertaining speeches. The selections presented in this volume form Cicero's main narrative of the crimes committed by Oppianicus the Elder and Sassia; it is easy to detach ourselves from the events set out by Cicero (since they happened well over 2,000 years ago), but it is worth remembering that this is a real court case; although Cicero surely exaggerates to influence his intended audience, it is chilling to think that these characters we read about were living people who may have done such terrible things in the fall-out of devastating civil wars.

This edition contains a detailed introduction to the context of the *Pro Cluentio*, supported by an in-depth summary of the controversy in the lead up to the trial. The notes to the speech itself aim to help students bridge the gap between GCSE and AS Level Latin, and focus therefore on the harder points of grammar, word order and sentence length. At the end of the book is a full vocabulary list for all the words contained in the prescribed sections, with words in OCR's Defined Vocabulary List for AS Level Latin flagged by means of an asterisk.

Matthew Barr

June 2019

Introduction

The life of Cicero

Marcus Tullius Cicero (106–43 BC) was a famous statesman and orator during the turbulent first century BC. He was born into an equestrian family in the municipality of Arpinum, but rose through the political ranks to become consul, the highest position in Rome, in 63 BC. This meant that Cicero was a *novus homo* – a 'new man' – who had come from humble backgrounds to seize the top political power (at the youngest age then possible). Cicero, even in his own day, was hailed as one of the greatest orators in Rome. His success as a lawyer was also widely known. He started his legal career towards the end of the 80s BC, and his most famous prosecution (against Verres, the former governor of Sicily) occurred in 70 BC.

Cicero was a Republican, which ultimately led to his downfall. Although not particularly interested in military life, he served with Sulla during the Social War (91–88 BC). He sided with Pompey during the civil war between Pompey and Caesar, but was later pardoned by Caesar for this. After Caesar's assassination in 44 BC, Cicero expressed his approval of the actions of the 'liberators' (Caesar's assassins). Cicero had never been close to Mark Antony, Caesar's right-hand man, and this approval secured their enmity. Having denounced Mark Antony in a famous set of speeches (the *Philippics*), Cicero found himself the target of the proscriptions (death sentences) of the Second Triumvirate. He was killed on 7 December 43 BC.

The trial to which the *Pro Cluentio* belongs occurred at a time when Cicero was at the height of his powers, the most famous orator in the Roman world; in fact, Cicero had been elected praetor for the same year and had gained significant political influence. It is an example of refined style and impressive legal rhetoric; it is persuasive and considered.

The trial in which the *Pro Cluentio* was given

Roman trials were between two private citizens. Both the accuser and the accused had the right to hire an advocate to speak on their behalf, and the case would be made in front of a presiding judge, agreed on by both parties, and a council of jurors to help the decision-making process. The judge was a private individual and would not necessarily have any training in legal matters (which is why the jury would be useful, for wider opinions and a more diverse knowledge of the law). Testimonies could be brought into court either in person or in writing, and by either side. The advocates arguing the case had no strict guidelines to which to adhere; character assassinations and appeals for pity were very common. The Roman state had no involvement, except in helping to appoint the judge and ensuring that the decision of the judge was upheld. Therefore, Roman trials were often very personal affairs.

In 66 BC, Aulus Cluentius Habitus was brought to trial by Statius Albius Oppianicus the Younger. Cluentius was charged with the following:

- bribing the jury at a previous trial of Oppianicus' father in 74 BC;
- poisoning Oppianicus' father in 72 BC;
- and attempting to poison Oppianicus, as well as successfully poisoning two others.

Cluentius hired Cicero alone to be his advocate in the trial and Cicero delivered one of his rhetorical masterpieces; although the result of the trial is not known for certain, it seems from the evidence available that Cluentius was acquitted. Oppianicus the Younger hired Titus

Accius to be his lawyer. In Roman trials, the prosecution delivered their speech first, and the defence delivered their speech after. Cicero's speech implies that Titus Accius had divided his prosecution into two main sections: the alleged bribery and the alleged poisonings. Cicero therefore deals with each in turn.

The previous trial of Oppianicus the Elder

The previous trial in 74 BC was brought against Statius Albius Oppianicus the Elder by Cluentius: Oppianicus the Elder was charged with having attempted to poison Cluentius through the use of two agents: Fabricius and Fabricius' freedman, Scamander. Cluentius had brought both to prosecution before he tried Oppianicus the Elder, and both Fabricius and Scamander had been found guilty. Scamander received one vote for acquittal (the juror Staienus gave this verdict) whereas Fabricius was unanimously condemned (especially after he ran out of the courtroom in fear before the end of his trial). With these two agents tried, Cluentius went after the mastermind, Oppianicus the Elder.

The trial of Oppianicus the Elder was very famous and divisive. Oppianicus the Elder was convicted by 17 votes to 15 (the jury consisting of 32 men). Of the 15 votes against conviction, ten were votes of *non liquet* ('not proven') and five were for acquittal. There was immediate suspicion of bribery and Cluentius was the subject of rumours that he had bribed jurors to obtain the conviction of Oppianicus the Elder. This trial, chaired by Gaius Iunius, became a tale of such infamy that several jurors were accused of judicial bribery and Cluentius was vilified amongst the Roman people. Therefore, when Oppianicus the Younger and Titus Accius came to prosecute Cluentius, they included this judicial bribery in their charges and tried to use Cluentius' blackened character against him.

Cicero makes a staggering defence of Cluentius and spends the majority of his speech defending his client on this charge rather than the charge of poisoning. Cicero has two refutations of the former charge: firstly, Oppianicus the Elder was certainly a guilty man, and any jury would have convicted him, so there was no need for Cluentius to bribe them; secondly, there was bribery at the trial of Oppianicus the Elder, but it was practised not by Cluentius but by Oppianicus the Elder. (Cicero's exploration of the crimes of Oppianicus the Elder will be dealt with shortly [see p. 5].) Cicero makes a stunning rhetorical statement to confound the jury: if bribery had been practised at the trial of Oppianicus the Elder (which it undoubtedly had), then it must either be by Cluentius or by Oppianicus the Elder; therefore, it is Cicero's job to prove that Oppianicus the Elder was the one who (unsuccessfully) bribed the jury, and by doing so he would absolve Cluentius. There is, of course, a problem with this logic which Cicero is hoping no one will notice: it is perfectly possible that *both* Cluentius *and* Oppianicus the Elder bribed members of the jury. Proving that Oppianicus the Elder practised bribery does not necessarily absolve Cluentius.

From a modern perspective, it seems very likely that Cluentius did bribe the jury at the trial. The story which Cicero unfolds shows Oppianicus the Elder giving Staienus (whom he thought most likely to be on his side after his vote in Scamander's trial) 640,000 sesterces to use to bribe 16 jurors (40,000 sesterces each); these votes, along with that of Staienus, who would expect more pay, would secure him a majority and, therefore, acquittal. Cicero claims that Staienus wanted to keep all 640,000 sesterces for himself and therefore promised money to other members of the jury but did not deliver it. Since the jurors did not receive their promised money, it was easy for Staienus to convince them that they had been deceived by Oppianicus the Elder and that they should vote for conviction. In this way, Staienus could keep all the money, since Oppianicus the Elder, as an exile, would not be able to prosecute him. This is Cicero's claim. It seems more likely, though, that Cluentius bribed Staienus and others with more money than Oppianicus the Elder had offered. Certainly this would explain the boast which Quintilian claims Cicero made: *se tenebras offudisse iudicibus in causa Cluenti gloriatus est* – 'he boasted that he had thrown dust in the eyes of the jury in the trial of Cluentius' (*Inst.* 2.17.21).

So, Cicero claims that Cluentius was not guilty of bribery in the previous trial. He also appeals to a technical legal issue: the law under which Cluentius is currently being tried (in 66 BC) applies only to men of senatorial rank; but Cluentius is of the equestrian order and therefore the law does not apply to him. Cicero says in his speech that Cluentius did not want to be defended by this technicality, but rather he wanted to be proven innocent, which is why Cicero only mentions it in passing. Naturally, we can assume that this claim is a further part of Cicero's rhetorical argument, attempting to persuade the jury that his client is innocent and does not need to hide behind legal loopholes, whilst at the same time pointing out a legal loophole.

The crimes of Oppianicus the Elder as related by Cicero

One of the most fascinating things about this speech is the list of crimes of which Oppianicus the Elder is apparently guilty. Cicero lays on the horrors thickly in his attempt to prove that any jury would have convicted such a guilty man, with the result that Cluentius had no reason for bribery. Cicero hopes in this way to convince the jury that the previous trial's verdict was a just one.

In the municipality of Larinum (south-east of Rome), there were three very wealthy families: the Cluentii, the Oppianici and the Aurii. Oppianicus the Elder wanted all the money of all three of these families for himself. To gain this money, he would have to commit or arrange the murders of no fewer than 11 people and marry 5 women. It is important to remember that Cicero is painting Oppianicus the Elder in the worst possible light, and some of these crimes are no doubt exaggerated (otherwise – why was he never brought to trial before?); Cicero presents Oppianicus the Elder as an absolutely despicable man who would stop at nothing to get at the money. Such character assassinations, absent from modern trials, were very common in Roman legal speeches.

Gaining the money of his own family was fairly easy. Oppianicus the Elder had one brother, Gaius Oppianicus, who was married to Auria (related to the Aurii household). Auria was pregnant with Gaius' child, and Oppianicus the Elder decided that it was inconvenient for his brother to have a child with whom he would have to share inheritance; so, according to Cicero, he poisoned and killed Auria as she came close to giving birth. He then poisoned his brother. Thus, the entirety of the Oppianici fortune was his.

Oppianicus the Elder married Cluentia, the paternal aunt of Cluentius, in order to get himself involved in the Cluentii family. However, that seems not to have been advantageous because he soon killed his wife with poison. A while after the death of Cluentius' father, he conspired to marry Cluentius' mother (which he did manage in the end) and then poison Cluentius to gain the fortune of the Cluentii (which is why he was put on trial in 74 BC). However, that comes later in his plans. First, he decided to infiltrate the Aurii.

The Aurii had as their head an elderly woman called Dinaea; she had four children: Marcus Aurius, Numerius Aurius, Gnaeus Magius and Magia. Oppianicus the Elder married Magia, who gave birth to a son, Oppianicus the Younger. Magia died (of natural causes) as did Numerius Aurius. Marcus Aurius fought in the Social War and was missing presumed dead. Then Gnaeus Magius' wife, Papia, became pregnant, but Gnaeus Magius died before the birth of his child. He left his money to be divided between his nephew, Oppianicus the Younger, and his mother Dinaea, unless the birth of his child be successful. Oppianicus the Elder, seeing that he would obtain the inheritance through his son, paid Papia a sum of money to have her child aborted. Then he married her, and they had a child; the marriage did not last long, and they soon divorced.

A problem reared its head when an informer came to Dinaea to tell her that her son, Marcus Aurius, who had been presumed dead, was actually alive and had been captured and thrown into slavery. Dinaea called her relatives to her to ask them to find her one remaining child. After this, she fell ill and made a will leaving all her money to Marcus Aurius and Oppianicus the Younger. Oppianicus the Elder took his opportunity to ensure the inheritance for his son: he killed Dinaea, forged a different will and paid for the informer to be bribed and for another man to carry out the murder of the recently rediscovered Marcus Aurius. The relatives of Dinaea made their quest to find Marcus Aurius, despite the death of Dinaea, but were led astray by the informer. They sent letters back to Larinum to say that the task was difficult because they understood that Oppianicus the Elder had bribed the informer. A relative of the Aurii, Aulus Aurius, claimed openly in the forum of Larinum that he would prosecute Oppianicus the Elder if Marcus Aurius were found dead. Marcus Aurius was indeed found dead, and Oppianicus the Elder fled Larinum to a camp of one of Sulla's generals. Using the uncertainty of Sulla's second civil war (83–81 BC), Oppianicus the Elder returned to Larinum, claiming that orders had been given to him by Sulla to declare martial law and proscribe certain members of the community. Proscription was a process of listing those members of the community who were to be killed. Amongst those for proscription were Aulus Aurius (who had threatened legal action against him), Aulus Aurius Melinus (the second husband of Sassia, Cluentius' mother) and his son Gaius Aurius, and Sextus Vibius, whom Oppianicus the Elder had used to bribe the informer.

With this rather sickening onslaught, Oppianicus the Elder had managed to gain the wealth of the Aurii. He married a fourth woman, Novia, about whom we know little apart from the fact that she bore him a son. The marriage clearly did not last long because he now set his sights on Sassia, the mother of Cluentius. Cicero takes pains to portray Sassia as a vicious woman who has a deep hatred of her own son; it is her, according to Cicero, who is pulling the strings behind the current trial. One of the first things we are told in this speech is about Sassia's rather unusual choice of a second husband. After the death of Cluentius' father, Cluentia (Cluentius' sister and, therefore, Sassia's daughter) married Aulus Aurius Melinus. Sassia fell in love with this man (her son-in-law) and, according to Cicero, 'bewitched his mind'. Subsequently, Aulus Aurius Melinus divorced Cluentia and married Sassia. It should be noted that Aulus Aurius Melinus later became a victim of Oppianicus the Elder.

Oppianicus the Elder began to woo Sassia. She seemed unconcerned with the fact that he had been responsible for the death of her second husband, but she did object to his bringing three children to the marriage: Oppianicus the Younger (born of Magia) and two further sons (born of Papia and Novia). Oppianicus the Elder decided that this should not cause too much of an issue. Oppianicus the Younger was the heir to Dinaea's fortune and therefore needed to be kept alive; the other two, though, seemed inconsequential. As a result, he had two of his own infant children murdered. Sassia seemed happy with this arrangement and therefore agreed to marry him. In the background to all this, Oppianicus the Elder had also arranged to have a young man named Asuvius murdered after forging his will to leave all the money to him. Needless to say, Oppianicus the Elder had racked up a serious amount of money through his crimes, according to Cicero.

The last part of the plan was to kill Cluentius. After Cluentius' death, all the money would belong to Sassia. Cicero also implies that Oppianicus the Elder would not have been averse to killing Sassia to ensure that all the money was his and only his. Unfortunately for Oppianicus the Elder, his plan was discovered through the slave of Cluentius' doctor. This slave, called Diogenes, was approached by the freedman Scamander (on the orders of Oppianicus the Elder) to administer poison to Cluentius while the doctor, Cleophantus, was treating him. Diogenes immediately reported this to Cleophantus, who in turn discussed the issue with Cluentius. It was decided that Cluentius would buy Diogenes in order to find out all the information pertaining to the plot and to catch Scamander red-handed. This plan worked, and Cluentius brought Scamander, then Fabricius (Scamander's patron), then Oppianicus the Elder to trial. Oppianicus the Elder was convicted and exiled.

The alleged poisonings

Cicero deals very briefly with the poisoning charges, considering them ridiculous. He instead chooses to focus on the animosity of Sassia towards Cluentius. Cluentius has been charged with poisoning Oppianicus the Elder and with attempting to poison Oppianicus the Younger (poisoning two others, Vibius Cappadox and Balbutius, also). Cicero deals with the poisoning of Vibius Cappadox and Balbutius very quickly, using the evidence of witnesses to prove his case (including Balbutius' own father). The attempted poisoning of Oppianicus the Younger is hardly addressed by Cicero; the attempted poisoning was supposedly intercepted by Balbutius (which is how he was poisoned), but since the evidence against the poisoning of Balbutius is so strong, it seems pointless to dwell on the attempted poisoning of Oppianicus the Younger. The attempted poisoning of Oppianicus the Elder is dealt with in slightly more detail.

Immediately after the death of her husband, Sassia wanted to pin his death on her son, Cluentius. She purchased the slave of Oppianicus the Elder's doctor, just like Cluentius had purchased Diogenes (see above). She had this slave, Strato, and another slave of Oppianicus the Elder, Nicostratus, tortured to try to get some admission of Cluentius' guilt out of them. Neither revealed any sort of plot by Cluentius. Indeed, Cicero claims that Oppianicus the Elder died after falling from his horse when already in a poor state of health. Sassia had to bide her time from that point onwards. Strato, who was the slave she had accused of being in on the plot of Cluentius to murder her husband, was rewarded by her with a shop. He later did not repay her kindnesses and robbed her, murdering two slaves in her household. Using this as an excuse, Sassia again tortured Strato (and Nicostratus) to try to exact some information out of them regarding Oppianicus the Elder's death. Again, she seemed not to get the result she wanted; so, according to Cicero, she forged the testimony of Strato and then cut out his tongue and crucified him. It was on this evidence that Cluentius was finally brought to trial. Cicero mocks the forgery and shows shock at the gall of the prosecution for bringing such an obviously forged document into the court. He considers the alleged poisonings to be completely ridiculous and hardly worthy of attention.

Structure of the speech

The main body of Cicero's speech is split into two sections, dealing in turn with the two main charges against Cluentius. As is usual in a Roman lawyer's speech, there is also an introduction and a conclusion. Below is the main structure of the speech; the section numbers given for this are based on the Oxford Classical Text (OCT) edition of the text.

Introduction (Sections 1–8)

Cicero introduces his defence by telling the members of the jury that he will answer Titus Accius' speech by using the same structure: by splitting his own into two parts. The first part of the speech will deal with the ill-feeling produced by the trial of Oppianicus the Elder and the second with the charges of poisoning. Cicero claims that the second part of his speech will be far shorter, but that the first part will be a lengthier exploration, seeing as it has been the subject of much misunderstanding and the cause of misdirected prejudice. Cicero appeals to the jury to forget their preconceptions and to give Cluentius a fair trial.

First part of the speech – Judicial bribery (Sections 9–160)

Introduction (Section 9): Cicero claims that he is going to use two strands to deal with the issues of the trial of Oppianicus the Elder: (1) he will show that Oppianicus the Elder was guilty; (2) he will show that bribery was practised by Oppianicus the Elder, not by Cluentius.

The crimes of Oppianicus (Sections 10–42): Cicero starts by exploring Sassia's behaviour (Sections 11–18) before moving on to a list of the crimes of Oppianicus the Elder (Sections 19–42).

The attempted poisoning of Cluentius (Sections 43–48): Cicero explains the motives of Oppianicus the Elder, the plan and how it was detected.

The convictions of Scamander and Fabricius (Sections 49–61): Cicero tells the jury of the easy convictions of Scamander and Fabricius, which significantly implicated Oppianicus the Elder. It should be noted that Cicero defended Scamander at his trial and has to explain to the jury why he took on the case of a man whom he now claims was completely guilty.

The trial of Oppianicus the Elder (Sections 62–87): Since his accomplices had been convicted, Oppianicus the Elder had every reason to bribe the jury, whereas Cluentius had none. Cicero now recounts the story of Oppianicus the Elder's bribery of Staienus and Staienus' greed in keeping the money for himself. Cicero claims that proof is available in Oppianicus the Elder's account books which show an unexplained

640,000 sesterces being paid out, which was a perfect amount to bribe 16 jurors.

Rebuttal of evidence of jurors which supported bribery theory (Sections 88–142): Cicero now embarks on a lengthy explanation of how the trials of the jurors involved in the trial of Oppianicus the Elder do not mean that Cluentius is guilty. Cicero also retracts what he himself had previously said about the trial of Oppianicus the Elder (which Titus Accius had clearly quoted at him) because, at the time, he had been ignorant of the facts of the case.

Technical legal discussion (Sections 143–160): Cluentius does not want to be defended on a legal technicality, but Cicero feels that he would not be doing his job if he did not mention the fact that the law under which Cluentius is being tried for judicial bribery does not, in fact, apply to him since he is not of senatorial rank.

Second part of the speech – The alleged poisonings (Sections 161–194)

Evidence of the character of Cluentius (Sections 161–164): Cicero deals with the character assassination of Cluentius, which has been going on since the trial of Oppianicus the Elder eight years previously. Cicero, of course, refutes these aspersions on the character of Cluentius.

The poisonings of Vibius Cappadox and Balbutius (Sections 165–168): Cluentius is innocent of these two poisonings, and Cicero relies on the testimony of witnesses, including Balbutius' own father, to prove this. Cluentius is said to have poisoned Balbutius by accident, the intended target being Oppianicus the Younger. However, if Cluentius is innocent of having poisoned Balbutius, he is also innocent of having made an attempt on the life of Oppianicus the Younger.

The murder of Oppianicus the Elder (Sections 169–194): Cluentius had no motive for killing Oppianicus the Elder, since he had been exiled and was living a terrible existence. The evidence implicating Cluentius is a complete forgery; the whole accusation was invented by Sassia, proof of his own mother's absolute hatred for her son.

Conclusion (Sections 195–202)

Cicero claims that Cluentius deserves the sympathy of the jury, given his mother's unnatural feelings towards him. The townsfolk of Larinum, and indeed others, show by their testimony and support that he is a commendable character. Cicero begs the jury to show mercy to Cluentius, who is completely innocent of all charges.

Literary style

The description of literary style has often been thought of as a tick-box exercise where spotting examples of figures of speech becomes the goal of reading a Latin passage and the easy refuge of a student facing an 'extended response' question. However, being able to spot stylistic features in itself does not do anything for our understanding of the speech or Cicero's motivations. One should always bear in mind, when reading anything, the author's potential intentions. In this speech, Cicero is attempting to persuade the jury of the innocence of Cluentius and to prove his arguments with factual references. Therefore, when noticing a particular literary feature, the first question should always be: how does this feature support Cicero's argument? The answer could vary: perhaps it is drawing attention to a particular piece of evidence; perhaps it is making a persuasive appeal to the emotions of the jury; perhaps it is highlighting the good character of Cluentius or the evil nature of Oppianicus the Elder or Sassia. The key is to explain how a feature enriches Cicero's speech; if you cannot think of a way in which a literary feature adds to Cicero's argument, then you should avoid mentioning it. The jury did not have a list of literary features which they were listening out for and they were not intending to acquit Cluentius if Cicero used enough alliteration; it is what the alliteration draws attention to which is the important thing. Similarly, the smaller components may not be all that contributes to the overall success of a speech: consider the way sentences are structured, the length of sentences or the rhythm of the words. It is often a composite of many different factors which creates a truly persuasive piece of rhetoric.

Therefore, when reading the *Pro Cluentio*, it is most important that you understand what Cicero means before you start 'analysing' the text. You do not have to understand any Latin to spot that *non* starts six successive clauses; but you do have to understand what Cicero is saying in order to determine why he starts six successive clauses with *non*. Throughout the commentary, certain points of literary style are mentioned and the effect is explained; this is by no means an exhaustive list. There are many other examples in the text which have an equally or more important effect. It is up to you, as a student of Latin, to select points of style and to explain how they contribute to the speech as a whole.

Below is a glossary of technical terms which might prove useful when analysing style. However, remember the advice above and only use these terms when you have contemplated what effect a particular feature has. Similarly, if you cannot remember a 'technical term', then do not panic: it is far more important to explain how the feature works and what its purpose is.

alliteration/assonance is an instance of repetition of particular sounds to draw attention to a phrase or make it more memorable. Alliteration refers to the repetition of consonants (usually restricted to the beginnings of words, although some may use it for the repetition of consonants anywhere in a word); assonance is the repetition of vowel sounds.

anaphora is the repetition of a word or phrase at the beginning of successive clauses or phrases. The word does not necessarily need to be in exactly the same form each time. An obvious example from this speech is in Section 1: *non pudor, non pudicitia, non* *pietas, non macula familiae, non hominum fama, non filii dolor, non filiae maeror.*

antithesis is a contrast, usually made clear by the words or phrases in antithesis being very close to each other. One could make a point about the antithesis in the following phrase from Section 1: *tametsi in huic hostili odio et crudelitate est, mater, inquam, appellabitur*. The antithesis between Sassia's attitude to her son (*hostili odio et crudelitate*) and her relationship with him (*mater*) is made clearer by the positioning of the words close to each other.

apostrophe is a direct address to someone, shown in Latin by the vocative case. The person can either be present (Cicero constantly appeals directly to the jury, *iudices*, and also addresses Titus Accius and Oppianicus the Younger, e.g. in Section 35: *quid ais, Tite Acci?*) or absent (addressing the gods is common in hyperbolic exclamations, e.g. in Section 36: *di immortales*).

asyndeton is the removal of conjunctions from a list of words or clauses. This creates speed and also the effect of a never-ending list. An example from the current text, which combines anaphora (above), can be found in Section 27: *nemo recipere tecto, nemo adire, nemo alloqui, nemo aspicere vellet?* By leaving out the conjunctions, Cicero makes the list feel longer.

chiasmus is a figure of speech where the word order is reversed in two similar clauses. It often allows words to be juxtaposed for emphasis, e.g. in Section 2: *vim deorum, hominumque famam*. The order of the first clause (accusative, genitive) has been reversed in the second clause (genitive, accusative); Cicero has therefore contrasted the words for gods and humans, showing how Sassia's behaviour has offended the whole realm of immortals and mortals.

exclamatio is some form of exclamatory statement. It is usually short and followed by an exclamation mark. Cicero uses quite a few of these in the *Pro Cluentio*, e.g. in Section 2: *o libidinem effrenatam et indomitam!*

hendiadys means 'one through two'. It is a common feature of Latin writing where two nouns (or sometimes verbs) are used in Latin where English would usually use an adjective and a noun (e.g. in Section 4, *clamore ac minis*: 'with a shout and threats' rather than the more natural English expression 'with loud threats').

hyperbole is exaggeration for an effect. For example, in Section 2 Cicero refers to Sassia's seduction of her son-in-law as *praeter hanc unam, in omni vita inauditum!* This is surely hyperbolic, since it is impossible to believe that Sassia is the first woman to fall prey to a passion for an inappropriate lover (compare the myth of Phaedra, with which Cicero would have been familiar).

isocolon is a repetition of clauses or phrases of similar lengths, usually, but not always, short. An example can be found in Section 31: *nulla vis tormentorum acerrimorum praetermittitur: aversari advocati et iam vix ferre posse: furere crudelis atque importuna mulier [. . .]*

juxtaposition is the placing together of two words for effect. In Latin literature, juxtaposition does not have to refer to two contrasting words (for which antithesis could be used); it refers to any two words which have been placed next to each other for emphasis. For example, in Section 2 Cicero says *discedit a Melino Cluentia.* Cluentia and her former husband have been juxtaposed to emphasize the horror of the divorce and Cluentia's sadness at leaving her husband.

litotes is a term for emphasis by understatement, usually involving a double negative. For example, in Section 35 Cicero says *quod nemo est Larinatium qui nesciat.* The use of *nemo est qui nesciat* ('there is no one who does not know') is equivalent to saying *omnes sciunt* ('everybody knows').

parallelism is when the word order of two similar clauses or phrases is the same. In this way, it is the opposite of chiasmus. In Section 2, Cicero refers to Cluentia when she leaves her husband Melinus: *ut in tantis iniuriis, non invita: ut a viro, non libenter.*

pleonasm is the use of more words than are necessary to convey the meaning of a phrase. This is not always an instance of being overly verbose, but is often intended for a purpose. You will find many examples in this text, but always think about what effect Cicero is trying to produce upon his listeners.

polyptoton is the repetition of a word in different forms. This could be a verb, noun and adjective of a common root repeated in their different word types or a particular word repeated in different grammatical forms (e.g. a noun in the nominative, then the accusative cases). A good example of this feature occurs in Section 7, when Cicero describes the murder of Cluentia; he uses the words *morior* and *mors* repeatedly in three successive sentences: *mori . . . mortua est . . . mortem . . . morientis . . . mortuae* (the last three of these are all in the same sentence).

polysyndeton is the use of multiple conjunctions, linking together a list of words or clauses. It is the opposite of asyndeton and often has the purpose of slowing down the speech. Similar to asyndeton, it can also give the impression of a never-ending list. Consider, for example, in Section 11: *nihil tam remotum ab accusatione quam Cluentius, et natura, et voluntate, et instituta ratione vitae.* The polysyndeton at the end of this sentence slows down the speech and allows us to focus on how averse to accusation Cluentius was in every aspect of his character.

repetition is the use of a word or phrase on more than one occasion. It is often part of another literary technique, but can be used as a device in its own right. Cicero likes to litter his speeches with repetition (remember, he is trying to convince a jury). An illustrative example comes in Section 1: *nam Sassia,* **mater** *huius Habiti –* **mater** *enim a me in omni causa, tametsi in hunc hostili odio et crudelitate est,* **mater**, *inquam, appellabitur: – ea igitur* **mater** *Habiti [. . .].*

rhetorical question is when a question is asked for a certain effect. Often rhetorical questions are explained as 'questions which expect no answer'; but since Cicero is delivering a speech in court, no question he asks will get an answer. The effect in rhetoric, then, is to force the audience to supply an answer in their own mind and therefore turn the question into a statement: e.g. in Section 4, *quis est, qui illum absolvi posse arbitraretur?* Cicero is expecting our response to be *nemo*, and so the question actually becomes a statement: *nemo est, qui illum absolvi posse arbitraretur.*

tautology is the use of two or more words with the same meaning, e.g. in Section 4: *his rebus in causa iudicioque patefactis. causa* and *iudicio* both have the meaning of 'trial' here.

tricolon is a literary effect where three similar clauses, phrases or words are linked, usually with the effect of crescendo (building up to the last clause). Tricola are often accompanied by other literary techniques such as anaphora. An example comes in the very first sentence of this edition: *erat . . . virtute, existimatione, nobilitate facile princeps.* The tricolon of nouns in the ablative produces an aggrandizing effect for the dead Aulus Cluentius Habitus.

variatio is the use of different syntax or words in order to draw attention to a particular part of the speech. For example, in Section 36 Cicero starts three successive clauses in this way: *ab eodem scelere . . . eiusdem amentiae . . . ex eodem furore.* Instead of using *ab* and an ablative each time, he varies the structure using case and prepositions to maintain interest.

Further reading

Froude, J. A., 'Society in Italy in the Last Days of the Roman Republic', in *Short Studies on Great Subjects* (1877). This volume is available online and contains an engaging, although inaccurate, retelling of the story of the trial of the *Pro Cluentio.*

Grant, M., *Cicero: Murder Trials* (Penguin, 1975). This volume contains an English translation of the complete speech, with notes and introduction.

Grose-Hodge, H., *Murder at Larinum* (Bloomsbury, 1992). The edition from which this text is taken; Grose-Hodge gives useful notes on the grammar and history for those beginning to tackle Latin prose for the first time and provides a full vocabulary list.

Hoenigswald, G. S., 'The Murder Charges in Cicero's Pro Cluentio', in *Transactions and Proceedings of the American Philological Association, Vol. 93* (1962), 109–23. An interesting, scholarly article arguing that Cluentius may well have been guilty of the charges of murder levelled against him.

Peterson, W., *M. Tulli Ciceronis Pro A. Cluentio Oratio* (MacMillan and Co., 1952). A scholarly edition of the complete speech with a useful introduction and full commentary.

Text

1. Aulus Cluentius Habitus fuit, pater huiusce, iudices, homo non solum municipii Larinatis, ex quo erat, sed etiam regionis illius et vicinitatis, virtute, existimatione, nobilitate facile princeps. is cum esset mortuus, Sulla et Pompeio consulibus, reliquit hunc annos XV natum, grandem autem et nubilem filiam: quae brevi tempore post patris mortem nupsit Aulo Aurio Melino, consobrino suo, adulescenti in primis, ut tum habebatur, inter suos et honesto et nobili. cum essent hae nuptiae plenae dignitatis, plenae concordiae, repente est exorta mulieris importunae nefaria libido, non solum dedecore verum etiam scelere coniuncta. nam Sassia, mater huius Habiti – mater enim a me in omni causa, tametsi in hunc hostili odio et crudelitate est, mater, inquam, appellabitur: – ea igitur mater Habiti, Melini illius adulescentis, generi sui, contra quam fas erat, amore capta, primo, neque id ipsum diu, quoquo modo poterat, in illa cupiditate se continebat: deinde ita flagrare coepit amentia, ut eam non pudor, non pudicitia, non pietas, non macula familiae, non hominum fama, non filii dolor, non filiae maeror a cupiditate revocaret. animum adulescentis, nondum consilio ac ratione firmatum, pellexit iis omnibus rebus, quibus illa aetas capi ac deleniri potest. filia, quae non solum illo communi dolore muliebri in eiusmodi viri iniuriis angeretur, sed nefarium matris pelicatum ferre non posset, de quo ne queri quidem sine scelere se posse arbitraretur, ceteros sui tanti mali ignaros esse cupiebat: in huius amantissimi sui fratris manibus et gremio, maerore et lacrimis consenescebat.

2. ecce autem subitum divortium; quod solatium malorum omnium fore videbatur. discedit a Melino Cluentia; ut in tantis iniuriis, non invita: ut a viro, non libenter. tum vero illa egregia et praeclara mater palam exsultare laetitia, ac triumphare gaudio coepit, victrix filiae, non libidinis. itaque diutius suspicionibus obscuris laedi famam suam noluit: nubit genero socrus, nullis auspicibus, nullis auctoribus, funestis ominibus omnium.

o mulieris scelus incredibile, et, praeter hanc unam, in omni vita inauditum! o libidinem effrenatam et indomitam! o audaciam singularem! nonne timuisse, si minus vim deorum, hominumque famam, at illos ipsos parietes, superiorum testes nuptiarum? perfregit ac prostravit omnia cupiditate ac furore: vicit pudorem libido, timorem audacia, rationem amentia. tulit hoc commune dedecus iam familiae, cognationis, nominis, graviter filius: augebatur autem eius molestia quotidianis querimoniis et assiduo fletu sororis.

3. initium quod huic cum matre fuerit simultatis audistis. nunc iam summatim exponam, quibus criminibus Oppianicus[1] damnatus sit. atque ut intellegatis iis accusatum esse criminibus Oppianicum[1], ut neque accusator timere, neque reus sperare potuerit, pauca vobis illius iudicii crimina exponam: quibus cognitis, nemo vestrum mirabitur, illum, diffidentem rebus suis, ad Staienum atque ad pecuniam confugisse.

Larinas quaedam fuit Dinaea, socrus Oppianici[1]: quae filios habuit Marcum Aurium et Numerium Aurium et Gnaeum Magium, et filiam Magiam nuptam Oppianico[1]. Marcus Aurius adulescentulus, bello Italico captus apud Asculum, in Quinti Sergii senatoris, eius, qui inter sicarios damnatus est, manus incidit, et apud eum fuit in ergastulo. Numerius autem Aurius, frater eius, mortuus est, heredemque Gnaeum Magium fratrem reliquit. postea Magia, uxor Oppianici[1], mortua est; postremo unus, qui reliquus erat, Dinaeae filius, Gnaeus Magius, est mortuus. is fecit heredem illum adulescentem Oppianicum[2], sororis suae filium, eumque partiri cum Dinaea matre

Oppianicus[1] = Oppianicus the Elder
Oppianicus[2] = Oppianicus the Younger

iussit. interim venit index ad Dinaeam, neque obscurus neque incertus, qui nuntiaret ei filium eius, Marcum Aurium, vivere, et in agro Gallico esse in servitute. mulier, amissis liberis, cum unius filii recuperandi spes esset ostentata, omnes suos propinquos filiique sui necessarios convocavit, et ab iis flens petivit, ut negotium susciperent, adulescentem investigarent, sibi restituerent eum filium, quem tamen unum ex multis fortuna reliquum esse voluisset. haec cum agere instituisset, oppressa morbo est. itaque testamentum fecit eiusmodi, ut illi filio HS CCCC milia legaret, heredem institueret eundem illum Oppianicum[2], nepotem suum. atque his diebus paucis est mortua. propinqui tamen illi, quemadmodum viva Dinaea instituerant, ita, mortua illa, ad vestigandum Aurium cum eodem illo indice in agrum Gallicum profecti sunt.

interim Oppianicus[1], ut erat, sicuti multis ex rebus reperietis, singulari scelere et audacia, per quendam Gallicanum, familiarem suum, primum illum indicem pecunia corrupit, deinde ipsum Aurium, non magna iactura facta, tollendum interficiendumque curavit.

4. illi autem, qui erant ad propinquum investigandum et recuperandum profecti, litteras Larinum ad Aurios, illius adulescentis suosque necessarios, mittunt; sibi difficilem esse investigandi rationem, quod intellegerent indicem ab Oppianico[1] esse corruptum. quas litteras Aulus Aurius, vir fortis et experiens, et domi nobilis, Marci illius Aurii propinquus, in foro, palam, multis audientibus, cum adesset Oppianicus[1], recitat, et clarissima voce, se nomen Oppianici[1], si interfectum Marcum Aurium comperisset, delaturum esse testatur. interim brevi tempore illi, qui erant in agrum Gallicum profecti, Larinum revertuntur: interfectum esse Marcum Aurium renuntiant. animi non solum propinquorum, sed etiam omnium Larinatium odio Oppianici[1], et illius adulescentis misericordia, commoventur. itaque cum Aulus Aurius, is qui antea denuntiaret, clamore hominem ac minis insequi coepisset, Larino profugit, et se in castra clarissimi viri,

Quinti Metelli, contulit. post illam autem fugam, et sceleris et conscientiae testem, numquam se iudiciis, numquam legibus, numquam inermem inimicis committere ausus est: sed per illam Lucii Sullae vim atque victoriam, Larinum in summo timore omnium cum armatis advolavit: quattuorviros, quos municipes fecerant, sustulit: se a Sulla et alios praeterea tres factos esse dixit: et ab eodem sibi esse imperatum, ut Aurium illum, qui sibi delationem nominis et capitis periculum ostentarat, et alterum Aurium, et eius Gaium filium, et Sextum Vibium, quo sequestre in illo indice corrumpendo dicebatur esse usus, proscribendos interficiendosque curaret. itaque, illis crudelissime interfectis, non mediocri ab eo ceteri proscriptionis et mortis metu terrebantur. his rebus in causa iudicioque patefactis, quis est, qui illum absolvi posse arbitraretur?

5. atque haec parva sunt: cognoscite reliqua: ut non aliquando condemnatum esse Oppianicum[1], sed aliquamdiu incolumem fuisse miremini.

primum videte hominis audaciam. Sassiam in matrimonium ducere, Habiti matrem, illam, cuius virum Aulum Aurium occiderat, concupivit. utrum impudentior hic, qui postulet, an crudelior illa, si nubat, difficile dictu est. sed tamen utriusque humanitatem constantiamque cognoscite. petit Oppianicus[1], ut sibi Sassia nubat, et id magno opere contendit. illa autem non admiratur audaciam, non impudentiam aspernatur, non denique illam Oppianici[1] domum, viri sui sanguine redundantem, reformidat: sed quod haberet tres ille filios, idcirco se ab his nuptiis abhorrere respondit. Oppianicus[1], qui pecuniam Sassiae concupivisset, domo sibi quaerendum remedium existimavit ad eam moram, quae nuptiis afferebatur. nam cum haberet ex Novia infantem filium, alter autem eius filius, Papia natus, Teani Apuli, quod abest a Larino XVIII milia passuum, apud matrem educaretur, arcessit subito sine causa puerum Teano: quod facere, nisi ludis publicis, aut festis diebus, antea non solebat. mater nihil mali misera suspicans mittit. ille se Tarentum proficisci cum simulasset, eo ipso die puer, cum hora undecima in publico valens visus esset, ante noctem mortuus, et postridie, antequam luceret, combustus est. atque hunc tantum maerorem matri prius hominum rumor quam quisquam ex Oppianici[1] familia nuntiavit. illa, cum uno tempore audisset, sibi non solum filium sed etiam exsequiarum munus ereptum, Larinum confestim exanimata venit, et ibi de integro funus iam sepulto filio fecit. dies nondum decem intercesserant, cum ille alter filius infans necatur. itaque nubit Oppianico[1] continuo Sassia, laetanti iam animo et spe optima confirmato. nec mirum, quae se non nuptialibus donis, sed filiorum funeribus delenitam videret. ita quod ceteri propter liberos pecuniae cupidiores solent esse, ille propter pecuniam liberos amittere iucundius esse duxit.

6. sentio, iudices, vos pro vestra humanitate, his tantis sceleribus breviter a me demonstratis, vehementer esse commotos. quo tandem igitur animo fuisse illos arbitramini, quibus his de rebus non modo audiendum fuit, verum etiam iudicandum? vos auditis de eo, in quem iudices non estis: de eo, quem non videtis: de eo, quem odisse iam non potestis: de eo, qui et naturae et legibus satisfecit: quem leges exsilio, natura morte multavit. auditis non ab inimico: auditis sine testibus: auditis, cum ea, quae copiosissime dici possunt, breviter a me strictimque dicuntur. illi audiebant de eo, de quo iurati sententias ferre debebant: de eo, cuius praesentis nefarium et consceleratum vultum intuebantur: de eo, quem oderant propter audaciam: de eo, quem omni supplicio dignum esse ducebant. audiebant ab accusatoribus: audiebant verba multorum testium: audiebant, cum unaquaque de re a Publio Cannutio, homine eloquentissimo, graviter et diu diceretur. et est quisquam, qui, cum haec cognoverit, suspicari possit, Oppianicum[1] iudicio oppressum et circumventum esse innocentem?

7. acervatim iam reliqua, iudices, dicam, ut ad ea, quae propiora huius causae et adiunctiora sunt, perveniam. vos, quaeso, memoria teneatis, non mihi hoc esse propositum, ut accusem Oppianicum[1] mortuum; sed, cum hoc persuadere vobis velim, iudicium ab hoc non esse corruptum, hoc uti initio ac fundamento defensionis, Oppianicum[1], hominem sceleratissimum et nocentissimum, esse damnatum. qui uxori suae Cluentiae, quae amita huius Habiti fuit, cum ipse poculum dedisset, subito illa in media potione exclamavit, se maximo cum dolore mori: nec diutius vixit, quam locuta est: nam in ipso sermone hoc et vociferatione mortua est. et ad hanc mortem tam repentinam, vocemque morientis, omnia praeterea, quae solent esse indicia et vestigia veneni, in illius mortuae corpore fuerunt.

eodemque veneno Gaium Oppianicum fratrem necavit. neque est hoc satis: tametsi in ipso fraterno parricidio nullum scelus praetermissum videtur; tamen, ut ad hoc nefarium facinus accederet, aditum sibi aliis sceleribus ante munivit. nam cum esset gravida Auria, fratris uxor, et iam appropinquare partus videretur, mulierem veneno interfecit. post fratrem aggressus est: qui sero, iam exhausto illo poculo mortis, cum et de suo et de uxoris interitu clamaret, testamentumque mutare cuperet, in ipsa significatione huius voluntatis est mortuus.

8–9: Cicero relates Oppianicus the Elder's murder of a young man named Asuvius, in order to inherit his money. Due to judicial corruption, Oppianicus the Elder is absolved of the murder in court.

10. quid? aviam tuam, Oppianice[2], Dinaeam, cui tu es heres, pater tuus non manifesto necavit? ad quam cum adduxisset medicum illum suum, iam cognitum et saepe victorem, mulier exclamat se ab eo nullo modo velle curari, quo curante suos omnes perdidisset. tum repente Anconitanum quendam, Lucium Clodium, pharmacopolam circumforaneum, qui casu tum Larinum venisset, aggreditur, et cum eo duobus milibus HS, id quod ipsius tabulis tum est demonstratum, transigit. Lucius Clodius, qui properaret, cui fora multa restarent, simul atque introductus est, rem confecit: prima potione mulierem sustulit: neque postea Larini punctum est temporis commoratus. eadem hac Dinaea testamentum faciente, cum tabulas prehendisset Oppianicus[1], qui gener eius fuisset, digito legata delevit: et, cum id multis locis fecisset, post mortem eius, ne lituris coargui posset, testamentum in alias tabulas transcriptum, signis adulterinis obsignavit. multa praetereo consulto. etenim vereor, ne haec ipsa nimium multa esse videantur. vos tamen eum similem sui fuisse in ceteris vitae partibus existimare debetis. illum tabulas publicas Larini censorias corrupisse, decuriones universi iudicaverunt.

11. cum illo nemo iam rationem, nemo rem ullam contrahebat: nemo illum ex tam multis cognatis et affinibus tutorem umquam liberis suis scripsit: nemo illum aditu, nemo congressione, nemo sermone, nemo convivio dignum iudicabat: omnes aspernabantur, omnes abhorrebant, omnes, ut aliquam immanem ac perniciosam bestiam pestemque fugiebant. hunc tamen hominem tam audacem, tam nefarium, tam nocentem, numquam accusasset Habitus, iudices, si id praetermittere, salvo capite suo, potuisset. erat huic inimicus Oppianicus[1]: erat: sed tamen erat vitricus: crudelis et huic infesta mater: attamen mater. postremo nihil tam remotum ab accusatione quam Cluentius, et natura, et voluntate, et instituta ratione vitae. sed cum esset haec illi proposita conditio, ut aut iuste pieque accusaret, aut acerbe indigneque moreretur; accusare, quoquo modo posset, quam illo modo emori, maluit.

12–25: Cicero relates Oppianicus the Elder's attempt on Cluentius' life and the subsequent trials of Scamander, Fabricius and Oppianicus the Elder. Scamander and Fabricius are easily convicted, leading Cluentius to pursue Oppianicus the Elder. During his trial, Oppianicus the Elder attempts to save himself by bribing the jury, but it backfires, and he is convicted and exiled.

26: Cicero proves that Cluentius did not poison Balbutius, through the testimony of Balbutius' father; this also absolves Cluentius of the attempted murder of Oppianicus the Younger.

27. unum etiam mihi reliquum eiusmodi crimen est, iudices, ex quo illud perspicere possitis, quod a me initio orationis meae dictum est: quidquid mali per hos annos Aulus Cluentius viderit, quidquid hoc tempore habeat sollicitudinis ac negotii, id omne a matre esse conflatum. Oppianicum[1] veneno necatum esse, quod ei datum sit in pane per Marcum Asellium quendam, familiarem ipsius, idque Habiti consilio factum esse, dicitis. in quo primum illud quaero, quae causa Habito fuerit, cur interficere Oppianicum[1] vellet. inimicitias enim inter ipsos fuisse confiteor: sed homines inimicos suos morte affici volunt, aut quod metuunt, aut quod oderunt. quo tandem igitur Habitus metu adductus, tantum in se facinus suscipere conatus est? quid erat, quod iam Oppianicum[1] poena affectum pro maleficiis, eiectum e civitate, quisquam timeret? quid metuebat? ne oppugnaretur a perdito? an ne accusaretur a condemnato? an ne exsulis testimonio laederetur? sin autem, quod oderat Habitus inimicum, idcirco illum vita frui noluit, adeone erat stultus, ut illam, quam tum ille vivebat, vitam esse arbitraretur, damnati, exsulis, deserti ab omnibus? quem propter animi importunitatem nemo recipere tecto, nemo adire, nemo alloqui, nemo aspicere vellet? huius igitur vitae Habitus invidebat? hunc si acerbe et penitus oderat, non eum quam diutissime

Oppianicus[1] = Oppianicus the Elder
Oppianicus[2] = Oppianicus the Younger

A
Level

vivere velle debebat? huic mortem maturabat inimicus, quod illi unum in malis perfugium erat calamitatis? qui si quid animi et virtutis habuisset (ut multi saepe fortes viri in eiusmodi dolore), mortem sibi ipse conscisset, huic quamobrem id vellet inimicus offerre, quod ipse sibi optare deberet? nam nunc quidem quid tandem illi mali mors attulit? nisi forte ineptiis ac fabulis ducimur, ut existimemus illum apud inferos impiorum supplicia perferre, ac plures illic offendisse inimicos quam hic reliquisse: a socrus, ab uxorum, a fratris, a liberum Poenis actum esse praecipitem in sceleratorum sedem atque regionem. quae si falsa sunt, id quod omnes intellegunt, quid ei tandem aliud mors eripuit praeter sensum doloris?

28. age vero, venenum per quem datum? per Marcum Asellium. quid huic cum Habito? nihil: atque adeo, quod ille Oppianico[1] familiarissime est usus, potius etiam simultas. eine igitur quem sibi offensiorem Oppianico[1] familiarissimum sciebat esse, potissimum et suum scelus et illius periculum committebat? cur deinde tu, qui pietate ad accusandum excitatus es, hunc Asellium esse inultum tamdiu sinis? cur non Habiti exemplo usus es, ut per illum, qui attulisset venenum, de hoc praeiudicaretur? iam vero illud quam non probabile, quam inusitatum, iudices, quam novum, in pane datum venenum! faciliusne potuit quam in poculo? latius potuit abditum aliqua in parte panis quam si totum colliquefactum in potione esset? celerius potuit comestum quam epotum in venas atque in omnes partes corporis permanare? facilius fallere in pane (si esset animadversum) quam in poculo, cum ita confusum esset ut secerni nullo modo posset? 'at repentina morte periit.' quod si esset ita factum, tamen ea res, propter multorum eiusmodi mortem, satis firmam veneni suspicionem non haberet. si esset suspiciosum, tamen ad alios potius quam ad Habitum pertineret. verum in eo ipso homines impudentissime mentiuntur. id ut intellegatis, et mortem eius et quemadmodum post mortem in Habitum sit crimen a matre quaesitum, cognoscite.

A Level

29. cum vagus et exsul erraret, atque undique exclusus Oppianicus[1] in Falernum se ad Lucium Quinctium contulisset, ibi primum in morbum incidit ac satis vehementer diuque aegrotavit. cum esset una Sassia, et Sexto Attio quodam, colono, homine valenti, qui simul esse solebat, familiarius uteretur quam vir dissolutissimus, incolumi fortuna, pati posset; Nicostratus quidam, fidelis Oppianici[1] servulus, percuriosus et minime mendax, multa dicitur renuntiare domino solitus esse. interea Oppianicus[1] cum iam convalesceret, neque in Falerno improbitatem coloni diutius ferre posset, et huc ad urbem profectus esset (solebat enim extra portam aliquid habere conducti), cecidisse ex equo dicitur, et homo infirma valetudine latus offendisse vehementer, et, posteaquam ad urbem cum febri venerit, paucis diebus esse mortuus. mortis ratio, iudices, eiusmodi est, ut aut nihil habeat suspicionis, aut, si quid habet, id intra parietes in domestico scelere versetur.

30. post mortem eius Sassia statim moliri nefaria mulier coepit insidias filio: quaestionem habere de viri morte constituit. emit de Aulo Rupilio, quo erat usus Oppianicus[1] medico, Stratonem quendam, quasi ut idem faceret, quod Habitus in emendo Diogene fecerat. de hoc Stratone et de Ascla quodam servo suo quaesituram esse dixit. praeterea servum illum Nicostratum, quem nimium loquacem fuisse, ac nimium domino fidelem arbitrabatur, ab hoc adulescente Oppianico[2] in quaestionem postulavit. hic cum esset illo tempore puer, et illa quaestio de patris sui morte constitui diceretur; etsi illum servum et sibi benevolum esse et patri fuisse arbitrabatur, nihil tamen est ausus recusare. advocantur amici et hospites Oppianici[1] et ipsius mulieris multi, homines honesti atque omnibus rebus ornati. tormentis omnibus vehementissimis quaeritur. cum essent animi servorum et spe et metu tentati, ut aliquid in quaestione dicerent, tamen, ut arbitror, auctoritate advocatorum adducti, in veritate manserunt, neque se quicquam scire dixerunt.

A Level

31. quaestio illo die de amicorum sententia dimissa est. satis longo intervallo post iterum advocantur. habetur de integro quaestio: nulla vis tormentorum acerrimorum praetermittitur: aversari advocati et iam vix ferre posse: furere crudelis atque importuna mulier, sibi nequaquam, ut sperasset, ea, quae cogitasset, procedere. cum iam tortor atque essent tormenta ipsa defessa, neque tamen illa finem facere vellet, quidam ex advocatis, homo et honoribus populi ornatus et summa virtute praeditus, intellegere se dixit, non id agi, ut verum inveniretur, sed ut aliquid falsi dicere cogerentur. hoc postquam ceteri comprobarunt, ex omnium sententia constitutum est, satis videri esse quaesitum. redditur Oppianico[2] Nicostratus: Larinum ipsa proficiscitur cum suis, maerens, quod iam certe incolumem filium fore putabat, ad quem non modo verum crimen sed ne ficta quidem suspicio perveniret: et cui non modo aperta inimicorum oppugnatio sed ne occultae quidem matris insidiae nocere potuissent. Larinum postquam venit, quae a Stratone illo venenum antea viro suo datum sibi persuasum esse simulasset, instructam ei continuo et ornatam Larini medicinae exercendae causa tabernam dedit.

32. unum, alterum, tertium annum Sassia quiescebat, ut velle atque optare aliquid calamitatis filio potius quam id struere et moliri videretur. tum interim, Hortensio et Quinto Metello consulibus, ut hunc Oppianicum[2] aliud agentem, ac nihil eiusmodi cogitantem, ad hanc accusationem detraheret, invito despondit ei filiam suam, illam, quam ex genero susceperat, ut eum nuptiis alligatum simul et testamenti spe devinctum posset habere in potestate. hoc ipso fere tempore Strato ille medicus domi furtum fecit et caedem eiusmodi: cum esset in aedibus armarium, in quo sciret esse nummorum aliquantum et auri, noctu duos conservos dormientes occidit in piscinamque deiecit: ipse armarii fundum exsecuit, et HS*** et auri quinque pondo abstulit, uno ex servis, puero non grandi, conscio. furto postridie cognito, omnis suspicio in eos servos, qui non

A
Level

comparebant, commovebatur. cum exsectio illa fundi in armario animadverteretur, quaerebant homines, quonam modo fieri potuisset. quidam ex amicis Sassiae recordatus est, se nuper in auctione quadam vidisse, in rebus minutis, aduncam ex omni parte dentatam et tortuosam venire serrulam, qua illud potuisse ita circumsecari videretur. ne multa: perquiritur a coactoribus: invenitur ea serrula ad Stratonem pervenisse. hoc initio suspicionis orto, et aperte insimulato Stratone, puer ille conscius pertimuit: rem omnem dominae indicavit: homines in piscina inventi sunt: Strato in vincula coniectus est: atque etiam in taberna eius nummi, nequaquam omnes, reperiuntur.

33–34: Cicero tells the jury that Strato and Nicostratus were tortured once more as an inquiry into the burglary. However, Strato's testimony focusses on the alleged poisoning of Oppianicus the Elder instead of the burglary, proving that it is forged.

35. iam videtis, illam nefariam mulierem, iudices, eadem manu, qua, si detur potestas, interficere filium cupiat, hanc fictam quaestionem conscripsisse. atque istam ipsam quaestionem dicite quis obsignarit. unum aliquem nominate. neminem reperietis, nisi forte eiusmodi hominem, quem ego proferri malim quam neminem nominari. quid ais, Tite Acci? tu periculum capitis, tu indicium sceleris, tu fortunas alterius litteris conscriptas in iudicium afferes; neque earum auctorem litterarum, neque obsignatorem, neque testem ullum nominabis? et, quam tu pestem innocentissimo filio ex matris sinu deprompseris, hanc hi tales viri comprobabunt? esto: in tabellis nihil est auctoritatis.

quid istis hominibus factum est, Stratone et Nicostrato? quaero abs te, Oppianice[2], servo tuo Nicostrato quid factum esse dicas: quem tu, cum hunc brevi tempore accusaturus esses, Romam deducere, dare potestatem indicandi, incolumem denique servare quaestioni, servare his iudicibus, servare huic tempori debuisti. nam Stratonem quidem, iudices, in crucem esse actum exsecta scitote lingua: quod nemo est

A
Level

Larinatium qui nesciat. timuit mulier amens non suam conscientiam, non odium municipum, non famam omnium; sed, quasi non omnes eius sceleris testes essent futuri, sic metuit, ne condemnaretur extrema servuli voce morientis.

36. quod hoc portentum, di immortales, quod tantum monstrum in ullis locis? quod tam infestum scelus et immane, aut unde natum esse dicamus? iam enim videtis profecto, iudices, non sine necessariis me ac maximis causis, principio orationis meae de matre dixisse. nihil est enim mali, nihil sceleris, quod illa non ab initio filio voluerit, optaverit, cogitaverit, effecerit. nihil est ab Oppianico[1] sine consilio mulieris cogitatum: quod nisi esset, certe postea, deprehensa re, non illa ut ab improbo viro discessisset, sed ut a crudelissimo hoste fugisset, domumque illam in perpetuum, scelere omni affluentem, reliquisset. non modo id non fecit, sed ab illo tempore nullum locum praetermisit in quo non instrueret insidias aliquas, ac dies omnes ac noctes tota mente mater de pernicie filii cogitaret. quae primum ut istum confirmaret Oppianicum[2] accusatorem filio suo, donis, muneribus, collocatione filiae, spe hereditatis obstrinxit.

neque in eo solum diligens fuit, ut accusatorem filio suo compararet sed etiam cogitavit, quibus eum rebus armaret. hinc enim illae sollicitationes servorum et minis et promissis: hinc illae infinitae crudelissimaeque de morte Oppianici[1] quaestiones: quibus finem aliquando non mulieris modus sed amicorum auctoritas fecit. ab eodem scelere illae triennio post habitae Larini quaestiones: eiusdem amentiae falsae conscriptiones quaestionum: ex eodem furore etiam illa conscelerata exsectio linguae: totius denique huius ab illa est et inventa et adornata comparatio criminis. atque his rebus cum instructum accusatorem filio suo Romam misisset, ipsa paullisper, conquirendorum et conducendorum testium causa, Larini est commorata: postea autem, cum appropinquare huius iudicium ei nuntiatum est, confestim huc advolavit, ne aut accusatoribus diligentia,

A Level

aut pecunia testibus deesset; aut ne forte mater hoc sibi optatissimum spectaculum huius sordium atque luctus et tanti squaloris amitteret.

37. iam vero quod iter Romam eius mulieris fuisse existimatis? quod ego propter vicinitatem Aquinatium et Fabraternorum ex multis audivi et comperi; quos concursus in his oppidis, quantos et virorum et mulierum gemitus esse factos? mulierem quandam Larino adesse, atque illam usque a mari supero Romam proficisci cum magno comitatu et pecunia, quo facilius circumvenire iudicio capitis atque opprimere filium possit! nemo erat illorum, paene dicam, quin expiandum illum locum esse arbitraretur, quacunque illa iter fecisset: nemo quin terram ipsam violari, quae mater est omnium, vestigiis consceleratae matris putaret. itaque nullo in oppido consistendi potestas ei fuit: nemo ex tot hospitibus inventus est, qui non contagionem aspectus fugeret. nocti se potius ac solitudini quam ulli aut urbi aut hospiti committebat. nunc vero quid agat, quid moliatur, quid denique quotidie cogitet, quem ignorare nostrum putat? quos appellarit, quibus pecuniam promiserit, quorum fidem pretio labefactare conata sit, tenemus. quin etiam nocturna sacrificia, quae putat occultiora esse, sceleratasque eius preces et nefaria vota cognovimus, quibus illa etiam deos immortales de suo scelere testatur, neque intellegit, pietate et religione et iustis precibus deorum mentes, non contaminata superstitione neque ad scelus perficiendum caesis hostiis, posse placari. cuius ego furorem atque crudelitatem deos immortales a suis aris atque templis aspernatos esse confido.

A
Level

Commentary Notes

1

Aulus Cluentius Habitus: This is the name of both the defendant and his father. It is the father about whom Cicero is now talking.

huiusce: This is an emphatic form of *huius*: 'the father of this man here'. Cicero uses parts of *hic* to refer to Cluentius because he is present in the trial; presumably Cicero points to him at particularly dramatic moments.

iudices: This is vocative. Cicero regularly addresses the jury throughout the speech to draw their attention to important points or simply to involve them in the action.

homo . . . princeps: This sentence is rather confusing in its order and needs careful attention. Cicero claims that his client's father was **facile princeps homo** of his own town and in further regions. Cicero uses the ablative of description, and a tricolon, to tell us in what regard Cluentius' father was the best: **virtute, existimatione, nobilitate**: 'in courage, reputation and standing'. The order of the sentence allows Cicero to emphasize the phrase **facile princeps** by leaving it until the end.

non solum . . . sed etiam: 'not only . . . but also'. This phrase draws attention to the impressive reputation Aulus Cluentius Habitus enjoyed.

municipii Larinatis: A *municipium* is a town which enjoyed the rights of Roman citizenship but was governed by its own laws and elected its own magistrates. **Larinatis** is an adjective: Larinum (the modern town of Larino) was in Samnium, south-east of Rome.

ex quo erat: Literally: 'from which he was'; i.e. 'which is where he was from'. Cicero is explaining that Cluentius' father was from Larinum, but that his reputation extended beyond just his own town.

Sulla et Pompeio consulibus: This is an ablative absolute: 'with Sulla and Pompeius being the consuls'. The Romans dated their years by quoting the names of the consuls for that year. Sulla and Quintus Pompeius Rufus were consuls in 88 BC.

hunc annos XV natum: **hunc** refers to the younger Cluentius, Cicero's client. **natum XV annos** literally means 'born for fifteen years'. In English we should translate it as 'fifteen years old'.

filiam: This is the client's sister, Cluentia.

quae: An example of the connecting relative; translating as 'who' or 'which' is always inappropriate in English. Translate it as 'she'.

nupsit: This verb is used of women marrying men; it takes the dative case.

Aulo Aurio Melino: Aulus Aurius Melinus is related to the Aurii family, though he is not one of the key family members.

consobrino suo: Aurius Melinus and Cluentia were related; it was not unusual for Romans to betroth their daughters to family members to keep property and wealth within the extended family.

adulescenti . . . honesto . . . nobili: These words are all in the dative case in apposition to Aurius Melinus; they describe him.

in primis: 'amongst the first men'. Aurius Melinus' reputation gave him the honour of being well-thought of and even considered one of the best from his town.

ut tum habebatur: **habebatur** is being used metaphorically: 'he was being held', i.e. 'he was thought of'. The **tum** emphasizes that his reputation was high when he married Cluentia; however, Cicero's subsequent revelations about his behaviour call into question this opinion.

inter suos: Although Aurius Melinus is not the grammatical subject of the sentence, *suos* refers to his peers. Sometimes the reflexive adjective is used regardless of the grammar if the meaning is clear. The adjective is being used substantively as a noun.

cum: This is a concessive **cum** clause: translate as 'although'.

plenae dignitatis, plenae concordiae: Notice the anaphora to emphasize how happy the marriage was at first. *plenus, -a, -um* is followed by a genitive.

repente est exorta: Cicero uses **repente** to show the suddenness of the evil which ruined the marriage. Notice that he has also reversed the usual order of the third person perfect *exorta est* to emphasize the present tense verb **est**, lending a vividness to the arrival of this evil.

mulieris importunae nefaria libido: The chiastic word order (noun, adjective, adjective, noun) emphasizes the **mulieris** and the **libido** whilst also juxtaposing the two extremely negative adjectives **importunae** and **nefaria**. Cicero is already setting up the shocking revelation of who this *mulier* is.

verum etiam scelere: Cicero hints at what is to come with the use of the noun *scelus*. Incest, even by marriage, was considered a crime in Roman times.

coniuncta: This is nominative feminine and agrees with **libido**: 'combined with'.

mater huius Habiti: Although Oppianicus is a ruthless killer, Sassia is presented as the true villain of the story by Cicero. This is the culmination of his shocking revelation: Cluentia's own mother became her love rival.

mater enim . . . appellabitur: An exaggerated explanation of how Cicero can bear to call her 'mother'. Throughout his speech, Cicero often emphasizes the cruelty of her acts by calling her **mater**, accentuating her relationship with the son she wants to ruin.

in omni causa: **omni** is used where we might expect the more sensible *tota*. Translate: 'in the whole case'. Cicero sticks to his word (see note above).

in hunc: 'towards him'. **hunc** refers to Cluentius, Cicero's client.

hostili odio et crudelitate: **hostili** is an adjective agreeing with **odio**. These are ablatives of description: 'she has an enemy's hate and cruelty'.

inquam: By placing himself in the speech, Cicero makes it more personal. He invites the jury into his narrative and allows them to see his thought processes.

ea igitur mater: The use of **ea** emphasizes the relationship between Sassia and Cluentius again. Notice that he has now used the word **mater** four times in the last sentence.

ea igitur . . . continebat: A rather complex sentence. Sassia is the subject (**ea mater Habiti**) and she is described as **amore capta** ('captivated by love'). As is common in Latin, a noun which is dependent on another noun goes into the genitive case: 'captivated by the love of . . .' She is therefore in love with **Melini illius adulescentis**.

adulescentis: The continued use of this word emphasizes the youth of Aurius Melinus and therefore the inappropriateness of Sassia's obsession with him.

generi sui, contra quam fas erat: The use of **generi sui** ('her own son-in-law') emphasizes their relationship and once more points to how inappropriate a match it is. The subordinate clause uses **contra quam** as a conjunction: 'against what was right'. **fas** is used for things which are right by divine law; therefore Cicero is suggesting that what Sassia is doing is impious.

neque id ipsum diu: 'and that itself not for very long'. This phrase will make sense once Cicero completes his sentence with a main verb. His suggestion is that Sassia cannot keep her lust in check for very long at all.

quoquo modo poterat: 'in whatever way she could'.

in illa cupiditate se continebat: We finally arrive at the main verb, of which Sassia is the subject. 'she was restraining herself in that desire' = 'she restrained her feelings'.

ita . . . ut: This is a result clause and so **ita** should be translated as 'so' or 'to such an extent'.

flagrare: This verb is metaphorical. It signifies Sassia's burning passion for Aulus Melinus and suggests the strength and uncontrollable nature of it.

amentia: This is an ablative of instrument: 'with madness'.

eam . . . revocaret: This sentence is particularly effective:

- **eam** (Sassia) is the object of the verb **revocaret** at the end.
- **a cupiditate** (notice the repetition of *cupiditas* from the previous sentence) is what she cannot be called back from.
- The subjects of **revocaret** are expressed in a long anaphoric list which tells us all the reasons why Sassia should not pursue her lust; the fact that none of these can restrain Sassia shows us how immoral she really is.
- Notice the alliterative nature of the first three nouns (**non pudor, non pudicitia, non pietas**), drawing attention to these three Roman values.

AS

- Cicero then launches into a chiastic phrase (**non macula familiae, non hominum fama**) to accentuate her disregard for the opinions of others.
- Finally, Cicero produces the climax of his list in two parallel phrases referencing the children whom Sassia has so easily ignored (**non filii dolor, non filiae maeror**); notice that Cluentia is left until the end because, ultimately, she is the person most affected by this situation: her mother has stolen her husband.

non pudor, non pudicitia: **pudicitia** is the ideal quality of women in the Roman world, like *virtus* for men. **pudor** and **pudicitia** come from the same root word (an example of polyptoton) and have some distinct connotations as well as an overlap in meaning. It is worth considering why Cicero chooses to use both.

revocaret: Although this verb has plural subjects, Cicero chooses to keep it singular to give the effect that the verb is to be repeated with each nominative in his list, strengthening the sense of shock. Also, by using the singular, it brings into sharper focus the last nominative on the list, which highlights the sorrow of Cluentia in this situation.

animum adulescentis: This is the object of the verb **pellexit**. Sassia is the subject.

nondum consilio ac ratione firmatum: **firmatum** agrees with and describes Aulus Melinus' **animum**. **consilio ac ratione** refer to his wisdom and understanding, and therefore his maturity. The use of **nondum** again underlines the age gap between Sassia and Aulus Melinus.

pellexit: This verb ('enticed, coaxed') is rather evocative.

iis omnibus rebus, quibus: Sassia uses all the techniques she can think of to capture Aulus Melinus.

illa aetas: 'that generation'; the abstract is being used to refer directly to Aulus Melinus. Notice yet another focus on the age of Aulus Melinus.

capi ac deleniri: The use of the passive is important: it continues the theme of Sassia being the active predator going after her prey. This metaphor is continued with the use of the verb **capi**, and **deleniri** paints Aulus Melinus as the passive victim of some enchantress.

filia . . . cupiebat: The main clause of the sentence is *filia cupiebat ceteros esse ignaros sui tanti mali*. Within the main clause, Cicero gives us two subordinate clauses: **quae . . . non posset** and **de quo . . . arbitraretur**. These two clauses tell us the plight of Cluentia; notice that the verbs are in the subjunctive, which produce a causal (**quae . . . non posset**) and a generic *qui* clause (**de quo . . . arbitraretur**).

quae . . . non posset: This causal *qui* clause gives the reason why Cluentia does not want others to know: 'since she was not only tormented by . . . but she could not bear . . .' She is embarrassed by the fact that her husband is attracted to another woman, but even worse is that the woman is her own mother.

pelicatum: This word suggests a cohabitation without being married, implying an affair between Sassia and Aulus Melinus before he divorced Cluentia.

de quo . . . arbitraretur: This is a generic subjunctive, suggesting the general feeling of a person in the given situation: 'about which one may think that they cannot even complain without committing a sin.' This translation is rather verbose and could be better rendered: 'which made her think that . . .'

ceteros: Probably best translated as 'everyone else' rather than just 'others.'

amantissimi: Notice the superlative adjective to describe Cluentius. Cicero is contrasting Sassia's and Cluentius' behaviours: Cluentius' was appropriate as a brother looking after his sister; Sassia's was completely inappropriate and showed no familial love.

in . . . manibus et gremio: It is very common for the preposition and its intended noun(s) to be split by a genitive in this way. Presumably Cluentia needed a lot of consolation after what happened with her marriage, and her brother provided this for her. **in manibus et gremio** is used here to indicate a consoling hug.

maerore et lacrimis: 'with sorrow and tears'. **maerore** is repeated from earlier in this section and **lacrimis** is introduced to evoke the sympathies of the jurors and to accentuate Sassia's cruelty.

2

ecce autem: The use of **ecce** introduces fresh drama and makes the revelation sudden and shocking. Cicero also reveals the story in short, sharp sentences.

subitum divortium: Cicero omits the verb *erat* to allow a faster pace: 'There was a sudden divorce'.

quod: This is a connecting relative and refers back to the **divortium**.

solatium: Cicero introduces this as a solution before suggesting that this is only the start of the problem by the use of the verb **videbatur**: 'this seemed'.

fore: This is the future infinitive of the verb 'to be'; it is equivalent to *futurum esse*.

discedit: Notice the prominent position of the verb to emphasize it as well as the use of an historic present to make the action more vivid.

An historic present is the use of a present tense verb when referring to past events; the intention is to bring the action into sharper focus and make it feel like it is happening right now. Having moved his jury to sympathy for Cluentia, Cicero now paints an arresting picture of her departure from her marriage. This is made even stronger by the delaying of the subject, Cluentia, to allow a juxtaposition with her once-husband, Melinus.

ut . . . ut: These are both causal and explain her feelings at leaving. Translate as 'since she was . . . since she was'.

ut . . . libenter: Notice the balanced phrases and the contrast between them. This creates a huge amount of pathos for Cluentia: she is not unwilling to leave, because she has been so wronged; but she is not glad to leave, because she is leaving her husband. The use of litotes (emphasis by understatement) in **non invita** and **non libenter** is effective in bringing forth Cluentia's emotions.

illa egregia et praeclara mater: Cicero again emphasizes Sassia's relationship with Cluentia and Cluentius to emphasize the horror of the situation. He ironically refers to her as **egregia et praeclara** because her conduct proves her to be anything but.

triumphare: Roman generals would gain a triumph when their troops had killed a certain number of enemies in battle. Cicero uses this verb to suggest the audacity of Sassia, presenting her like a conquering general.

victrix filiae, non libidinis: The nouns **filiae** and **libidinis** are genitive because they are dependent on **victrix**: 'the conqueror of . . .' Cicero cleverly juxtaposes **victrix filiae**, showing the unnaturalness of the situation. He also suggests that Sassia should have conquered her lust and not her daughter, highlighting once again her bad behaviour.

diutius: The comparative of *diu*.

suspicionibus obscuris laedi famam suam: A sarcastic comment from Cicero; he suggests that Sassia was not happy having her reputation damaged by 'hidden suspicions', and so she revealed the suspicions to be true so that people could at least judge her correctly. Again, it highlights the boldness of Sassia.

nubit genero socrus: The verb, in the historic present, is promoted to the beginning of the clause to reveal how she displayed these 'hidden suspicions'. It also allows Cicero the opportunity to juxtapose **genero** and **socrus**, emphasizing the horror of the relationship and mirroring **discedit a Melino Cluentia** earlier to accentuate the comparison.

nullis . . . omnium: This tricolon shows the attendant circumstances for the wedding. The repetition of **nullis** emphasizes what they do not have (i.e. soothsayers and guardians, which should be attendant) and then a quick shift to what they do have (i.e. the deadly omens of everyone, which is not a great start for a marriage).

auctoribus: An *auctor* is someone to approve the wedding. The suggestion is that no one approved of this match.

o scelus . . . o libidinem . . . o audaciam: These are all accusatives of exclamation. The outburst must have excited the courtroom immensely, adding further drama to the situation. Cicero's disbelief is evident.

praeter hanc unam: A shorthand for the longer *praeter huius unius mulieris scelus*. The idea is that Cicero has never heard the like of such a crime from any other woman.

in omni vita: 'in all my life'.

effrenatam et indomitam: These two words suggest just how out of control Sassia has become and give an impression of the wildness of her lust.

nonne timuisse: The infinitive is being used because Cicero has slipped into an indirect statement (the accusative and infinitive construction). He uses it to highlight his indignation: 'Surely you would think that she feared . . .'

si minus . . . at: This draws a contrast: 'if not so much X, but certainly Y'.

vim . . . famam: Cicero points out two factors which should have caused Sassia to fear her actions and he draws attention to them by his use of chiasmus (juxtaposing **deorum** and **hominum** to show that both the immortal and mortal realm judge her harshly for her behaviour).

illos ipsos parietes: The **parietes** are particularly the walls between rooms in a house. Cicero personifies the walls and draws attention to them with two pronouns: 'those very walls themselves'. He then casts the walls as **testes** ('witnesses') to the former marriage (i.e. Aulus Melinus' marriage to Cluentia).

superiorum . . . nuptiarum: The genitive is used when a noun is dependent on another noun (as the **nuptiarum** is dependent on the **testes**). Quite often 'of' doesn't work as well in English. Whilst we could say 'witnesses of', we would more naturally say 'witnesses to'. Notice the clever positioning of **testes** between the adjective and noun, making the witnesses surrounded by the previous marriage.

perfregit . . . furore: The verbs have been promoted to give them an immediacy and increase the shock value; they are also emphasized by their alliterative quality and the fact that they are both compound verbs (*per+frango* and *pro+sterno*) which increases the force of them. Notice that Cicero balances the sentence with two verbs (joined by **ac**), the object (**omnia**) and two instrumental ablatives (again joined by **ac**).

vicit . . . tulit . . . augebatur: Cicero has promoted all the verbs in these clauses to the beginning to sharpen the conclusion of Sassia's actions and their effect on others.

pudorem . . . amentia: A tricolon of conquerors and defeated. **libido**, **audacia** and **amentia** are all the subject of **vicit** (which remains singular due to its proximity to **libido**; the listener is encouraged to imagine the word again in each successive clause, giving it greater emphasis). **pudorem**, **timorem** and **rationem** are the objects. Cicero contrasts opposites here: 'lust conquered modesty, recklessness conquered fear and madness conquered reason'. Notice as well that Cicero places the accusative before its nominative, perhaps to lend emphasis to the quality which should be upheld and to show the subversion of the natural order of things.

tulit . . . filius: **filius** is the subject and has been left until the end of the clause for emphasis. *graviter ferre* = 'to bear/take [something] badly'. **hoc commune dedecus** is in the accusative case and is the object. Cicero only gives us the adverb and the subject of the verb at the end of the clause; therefore, listening to him, a juror might be tempted to understand at first that 'Sassia' bore this dishonour 'easily' until given the full gravity of the situation by the introduction of the adverb and nominative.

familiae, cognationis, nominis: The nouns in this tricolon are in the genitive because they are dependent on **dedecus**: 'dishonour to his household, his kin and his name'. The list increases the sphere of dishonour from his immediate household through to his very name in the public eye.

augebatur . . . eius molestia: **molestia** is the nominative. **eius** (the genitive of *is*, *ea*, *id*) is used as a third person personal pronoun: 'his distress'. **augebatur** is passive: 'was being increased'.

quotidianis . . . sororis: The two adjectives, **quotidianis** and **assiduo**, emphasize how upset Cluentia is about what has happened. By leaving **sororis** until the end of the clause, Cicero evokes our pity for her and shows us the effect of Sassia's actions on her two children.

3

initium . . . audistis: **audistis** is a common syncopated (shortened) version of *audivistis*. Latin verbs can often be shortened by removing the *-ve-* or *-vi-* from the perfect stem. The verb is addressed to the jurors and introduces an indirect question: *quod initium simultatis fuerit huic cum matre*.

huic cum matre: **huic** is the dative of possession and refers to Cluentius: 'the beginning of his enmity with his mother'. In English, it might be better expressed as 'the beginning of the enmity between him and his mother'.

fuerit: This is the perfect subjunctive of the verb *esse*. It is in the subjunctive because it forms part of the indirect question.

simultatis: A *simultas* is any sort of hostile encounter between two parties.

nunc iam: Cicero often starts sentences with these two words to point out where his argument is moving to next: 'Now, indeed'.

summatim: The adverb suggests brevity, but Cicero is going to give us a lot of details about the charges against Oppianicus the Elder to prove just how nasty he really was.

exponam: Remember that Cicero is giving this speech in a courtroom, so the use of the first person is not unusual.

damnatus sit: This is the perfect passive subjunctive of *damno*: 'was condemned'.

atque . . . exponam: The main clause is **pauca vobis illius iudicii crimina exponam**. **pauca** agrees with **crimina**, which is neuter accusative plural. **illius iudicii** is genitive: 'of that trial' and references Cluentius' prosecution of Oppianicus the Elder (see Introduction).

ut intellegatis: This is a purpose clause dependent on the main verb **exponam**: 'I shall relate . . . so that you may understand'. **intellegatis** is present subjunctive because the clause is primary in sequence. The verb also introduces an indirect statement here.

iis . . . criminibus: These two words agree and are ablative.

accusatum esse . . . Oppianicum: Oppianicus the Elder is the subject of the indirect statement.

ut . . . potuerit: This is a result clause without the usual 'signpost' word. **ut** is best translated as 'with the result that'. Cicero says that the prosecutor was not able to be afraid and the defendant was not able to hope; his point is that the charges and evidence against Oppianicus the Elder were so great that the prosecutor (Cluentius) could not lose and the defendant (Oppianicus the Elder) could not win.

quibus cognitis: This phrase is an ablative absolute; **quibus** is a connecting relative: literally = 'with these things having been found out'. There are many better ways to express it in English, though.

nemo vestrum: **vestrum** is the partitive genitive of *vos*: 'none of you'.

illum: i.e. Oppianicus the Elder. He is the subject of the indirect statement.

rebus suis: 'his own matters'. Cicero suggests that Oppianicus the Elder could not rely on his own ability to get himself free of the charges.

ad Staienum . . . confugisse: Oppianicus the Elder is described as having fled to Staienus and money. (For Staienus, the corrupt juror, see Introduction). **ad pecuniam** = 'to bribery'.

Larinas: This is an adjective, not a noun: 'Dinaea was a woman of Larinum'.

Dinaea: See Introduction for an explanation of Dinaea's family and her relationship to Oppianicus the Elder.

bello Italico: The Social War (often called the Italian War) was fought between 91 and 88 BC. The Italians demanded Roman citizenship and won this for themselves in the culmination of the war.

apud Asculum: **apud** means 'in the vicinity of'. Asculum is a town in Picenum, to the north-east of Rome. It was the first city to rise against Rome in the Social War and there was a major battle in the town in 89 BC; the town was captured.

in Quinti Sergii . . . incidit: There is quite a lot going on in this sentence. Marcus Aurius is the subject of the main verb **incidit**. The preposition **in** governs **manus** (accusative plural): 'into the hands'. It is very common for a genitive to go between the preposition and the noun it governs, as it does here: **Quinti Sergii senatoris, eius**. However, this is made complicated by a relative clause referring to the senator Quintus Sergius, into whose hands Marcus Aurius has fallen. The word order tells us that the relative clause refers to Quintus Sergius.

inter sicarios: This is the technical legal term for a court which deals with murder trials. Quintus Sergius was convicted of murder.

apud eum: i.e. 'his'.

fuit: Marcus Aurius is the subject of this verb as well.

in ergastulo: A workhouse for slaves or convicted criminals.

heredem: This is in apposition to **Gnaeum Magium fratrem**: 'he left his brother Gnaeus Magius as his heir'.

is: This refers to Gnaeus Magius.

illum adulescentem Oppianicum: This refers to Oppianicus the Younger. Cicero uses the demonstrative pronoun **illum** because, as prosecutor, Oppianicus the Younger would be in the courtroom. He may well have even pointed him out at this juncture.

partiri: The infinitive from the deponent verb *partior*.

index: This word refers to anyone who points something out. It is probably best translated as 'informer'.

neque obscurus neque incertus: i.e. he is certain of what he knows and states it clearly and without doubt.

qui nuntiaret: Notice the relative pronoun used with a subjunctive to express purpose. This is a very common construction in Latin; translate **qui** as if it were *ut*.

filium . . . in servitute: An indirect statement after **nuntiaret**.

in agro Gallico: The Ager Gallicus was a region of land on the Adriatic coast of Italy stretching through Umbria and a small portion of Picenum.

mulier . . . voluisset: A long Ciceronian sentence. However, taken slowly it can be tackled pretty methodically. The key thing to do when faced with such a long sentence is keep the endings of words in mind and assess the function of each word in the sentence.

unius filii recuperandi spes: **spes** + genitive of gerund/gerundive = 'the hope of . . . ing'. The gerund is normally used, but when a gerund takes a direct object, as it does here ('the hope of recovering *her only son*'), a process known as gerundival attraction takes place. The gerund is replaced by a gerundive. It does not make a difference to our translation: 'the hope of recovering her only son'.

flens: Present participle agreeing with Dinaea (the subject of the sentence). Notice how Cicero again stirs up pity for this woman, who has lost all her children and now has the chance to regain one of them.

sibi: In a purpose clause, the reflexive is used to refer back to the subject of the main verb (in this case Dinaea) rather than the subjects of the verbs within the purpose clause.

tamen: The use of **tamen** indicates an unexpressed phrase: 'whom [although all her other children had died], however . . .'

unum . . . voluisset: **fortuna** is personified here, creating sympathy for Dinaea in her plight. The verb **voluisset** can mean 'had been willing' as well as 'had wanted'. *unus* can have the force of 'only' as well as 'one', and **ex multis** = 'out of many'. 'whom fortune had been willing to be the only one left out of many'.

haec: Neuter plural: 'these things'. Cicero is referring to Dinaea's actions in the previous sentence.

oppressa morbo est: Although it is tempting to translate **oppressa morbo est** as 'overcome by disease', it may be best to translate it as 'fell ill'. The details of her illness appear in Section 10.

ut . . . legaret: A purpose clause explaining the terms of Dinaea's will.

illi filio: Dative case after **legaret**. This refers to Marcus Aurius who has been discovered alive.

HS CCCC milia: '400,000 sesterces'. *mille* is indeclinable in the singular, but declines like a neuter third declension in the plural. **CCCC** is a Roman numeral = 400 (this is a common alternative to the subtractive version *CD*). **HS** stands for 'sesterces' (see note below).

It is difficult to convert Roman money into modern terms, but 400,000 sesterces might be somewhere between £200,000 and £300,000. A Roman citizen needed to own a fortune of 400,000 sesterces to become a member of the equites (‘knights’), so it is certainly not an insignificant sum, especially in a country town.

HS: This stands for *duo et semis* (‘two and a half’) because there are 2.5 asses (the smallest Roman coin) in one sestertius. The ‘H’ is not, in fact, the letter ‘h’ but it represents the Roman numeral for two (II) with a line through it; the symbol for a sestertius should be ‘~~HS~~’. However, when texts began to be printed, it was not easy to strike through letters, so ‘H’ was used to represent ‘~~H~~’.

eundem illum Oppianicum: Oppianicus the Younger whom Cicero mentioned a little earlier (hence **eundem**).

nepotem suum: Oppianicus the Younger is the son of Oppianicus the Elder and Magia (Dinaea’s daughter).

his diebus paucis: Ablative of time within which: ‘in a few days’.

est mortua: We shall see just how in Section 10. Cicero leaves it very vague for now, but he will reveal Oppianicus the Elder’s hand in the murder later on.

viva Dinaea . . . mortua illa: Both ablative absolutes describing the circumstances: ‘when Dinaea was alive . . . when she was dead’.

ad vestigandum Aurium: **ad** + gerund/gerundive = purpose: ‘(in order) to track Aurius’.

cum eodem illo indice: i.e. the informer who first came to Dinaea.

sicuti multis ex rebus reperietis: **sicuti** is a variant of *sicut*. **multis** agrees with **rebus** which is ablative after **ex. reperietis** is second person plural future tense of *reperio*: ‘you will discover’.

singulari scelere et audacia: Ablatives of description: 'since he was a man of extraordinary wickedness and impudence'.

per quondam Gallicanum: **per** is used here to express the person through which something is achieved. **Gallicanum** refers to a person from Gaul (roughly modern-day France), but here probably means a local of Ager Gallicus (see note on p. 50).

primum . . . deinde: 'Firstly . . . secondly'.

pecunia: Ablative of instrument: 'with money'.

ipsum Aurium: This refers to Marcus Aurius. He is the object of **tollendum interficiendumque curavit**.

non magna iactura facta: An ablative absolute: 'with no great loss having been made'. Cicero uses litotes to express how little it cost Oppianicus the Elder to get Marcus Aurius killed; this serves to increase the callous impression of Oppianicus the Elder: he was even cheap when doing away with his enemies.

tollendum interficiendumque curavit: *curo* + gerund/gerundive = 'to see to the . . . ing/to get [something] done'. *tollo* here means 'remove' rather than just 'raise'.

4

illi: Masculine nominative plural, the subject of the main verb **mittunt**: 'Those men'.

erant . . . profecti: Despite the long separation, this is a third person pluperfect tense of the deponent verb *proficiscor*.

ad propinquum investigandum et recuperandum: The gerund/gerundive of purpose (see p. 52); **propinquum** refers to Marcus Aurius.

Larinum: Cities and towns which take the locative case (including Larinum and Rome) do not take a preposition in Latin. This means 'to Larinum'.

ad Aurios: The *Aurii* (plural of Aurius) are the members of the family who are still in Larinum.

illius adulescentis: This is genitive and refers to Marcus Aurius. It qualifies **Aurios**: 'the Aurii, family members of that young man'.

suos necessarios: To be taken with **ad** earlier: 'and to their own friends/relatives'.

mittunt: An historic present (see note on **discedit** on p. 42). Note that the historic present counts as a past tense and therefore its sequence is historic (hence **intellegerent** in the imperfect subjunctive).

sibi . . . corruptum: **litteras mittunt** introduces an indirect statement even though there is no explicit verb of saying: 'They sent letters [which said] that . . .'

sibi: The reflexive refers back to the subject of the main verb, **mittunt**.

investigandi rationem: *ratio* is perhaps best translated as business in this context. **investigandi** is the genitive of the gerund: 'the business of investigating'.

quod intellegerent: Subordinate clauses within indirect statements use the subjunctive; the tense of the subjunctive is decided by the sequence of tenses (see note above on **mittunt**). **intellegerent** introduces another indirect statement: 'because they understood that . . .'

quas litteras: **quas** is the connecting relative: 'these letters'. It is the object of the main verb **recitat**. Note that, whilst *litterae* can mean a single letter, it is more likely to be plural because the letters were sent to the Aurii and the investigators' own friends.

Aulus Aurius: This man is the subject of the verb **recitat** and we are given lots of information about him. He is not Aulus Aurius Melinus, the ex-husband of Cluentia and the new husband of Sassia. The two are related, however.

vir . . . propinquus: Cicero tells us how outstanding a man Aulus Aurius is to contrast him with Oppianicus the Elder. He also tells us that he is a relative of Marcus Aurius, though he cannot be a brother since Marcus' brothers have all died by this time.

in foro, palam, multis audientibus: The forum was a place which the townsfolk would have frequented every day, so to read these letters in this very public space would have set rumours flying and the entire town would know about the situation very quickly. **multis audientibus** could be an ablative absolute ('with many people listening') or a dative after **recitat**: 'to the many listeners'.

cum adesset Oppianicus: Notice that Cicero draws attention to the fact that Aulus Aurius has the bravery to read these letters out in front of Oppianicus the Elder himself.

recitat: Notice the use of another historic present. Cicero litters these next sentences with historic presents to emphasize the action and reveal to us little by little what is happening in Larinum: **testatur . . . revertuntur . . . renuntiant . . . commoventur**.

se . . . testatur: **testatur** introduces an indirect statement. Aulus Aurius is the subject of the indirect statement, made clear by the reflexive pronoun **se**.

si . . . comperisset: The pluperfect subjunctive is used to represent the future perfect of the condition in direct speech. What Aulus Aurius actually said was: '*ego, si interfectum Marcum Aurium comperero, nomen Oppianici deferam*' – 'If I find [*lit.*: shall have found] Marcus Aurius murdered, I shall prosecute Oppianicus.'

nomen . . . delaturum esse: *nomen deferre* is a technical term meaning 'to accuse' or 'to prosecute'.

brevi tempore: Ablative of time within which: 'after a short time'.

Larinum: See note on p. 54.

animi: This is the subject of the verb **commoventur**.

non solum . . . sed etiam: Notice that Cicero emphasizes that it is not just Marcus Aulus' relatives who are affected by this news, it is the entire population of Larinum.

odio . . . misericordia: Cicero uses a chiasmus to emphasize the two men and the different reactions to them (**illius adulescentis** refers to Marcus Aurius).

commoventur: As in English, *commoveo* can be both literal ('to move something physically') or metaphorical ('to move someone emotionally').

denuntiaret: This is really shorthand for *nomen deferre nuntiaret*: 'had given notice of his intention to prosecute'. It is subjunctive because it suggests a causal link: because he had said that he was going to prosecute him, he now makes good on his threat.

clamore . . . ac minis: This is an example of hendiadys ('one through two'), a common figure of speech in Latin. Hendiadys expresses a single idea through two distinct nouns where in English we should expect an adjective and a noun: *lit.* 'with a shout and threats' = 'with loud threats'.

Larino: **Larino** = 'from Larinum' (see note on p. 54).

se . . . contulit: *se conferre* means 'to carry oneself to, to go'.

Quinti Metelli: Quintus Caecilius Metellus Pius was a general in the Social War and a great ally of Sulla's when he returned from the East in 83 BC.

et sceleris et conscientiae testem: The **testem** is being used in apposition to **fugam**. Oppianicus the Elder's flight is also a witness. **sceleris** refers to his guilt and **conscientiae** to his guilty conscience.

numquam . . . ausus est: Notice the anaphora of **numquam**, emphasizing Oppianicus the Elder's total isolation and lack of legal recourse.

per . . . victoriam: **per** is probably best translated here as 'taking advantage of' rather than 'through'. Oppianicus the Elder uses the cover of the violence and victory of Lucius Sulla to storm his way back into Larinum. Sulla took the role of dictator in 81 BC after his march on Rome and quickly purged the city of political rivals through his use of 'proscriptions' (see note on **proscribendos** on p. 59).

in summo timore omnium: **in** suggests the circumstances in which Larinum found itself: 'during everyone's utmost terror'.

advolavit: Cicero uses a metaphor ('flew at') to sharpen his comparison of Oppianicus the Elder with some terrible predator.

quattuorviros: The *quattuorviri* were a council of four elected magistrates charged with running a municipium. They were elected annually by the *municipes* (the townspeople).

fecerant: This verb means 'elected' or 'chose' here and is used to contrast with **factos esse** later on. Cicero is showing the horror of the democratically elected council being replaced by an unelected, despotic council.

sustulit: From *tollo*; whilst *tollo* can mean 'to kill', it is probably best translated as 'to remove'. Oppianicus the Elder deposes the old *quattuorviri* and replaces them with himself and three others.

dixit: Cicero implies that Oppianicus the Elder explained himself to the townspeople; Cicero clearly thinks that this is an excuse, seeing as he puts the words in Oppianicus the Elder's mouth, rather than Sulla's.

alios . . . tres: Oppianicus the Elder and these three other men have become the new *quattuorviri*. Translate **factos esse** as 'had been made [the council of four]' (and see note on **fecerant** above).

ab eodem: This refers again to Sulla.

sibi esse imperatum: Intransitive verbs (those which take no direct object, like *impero*) cannot easily be turned passive. However, Latin can use the 'impersonal passive' with such verbs: **imperatum est** means 'there was an order'. The person ordered then goes into the dative case (hence **sibi**). In English, it can simply be translated as 'he had been ordered . . .'

sibi: This refers to Oppianicus the Elder (the subject of the main verb).

ut . . . curaret: This is an indirect command expressing what it is that Oppianicus the Elder has been ordered to do by Sulla.

Aurium illum . . . alterum Aurium . . . Gaium . . . Sextum Vibium: These are the objects of the verb in the indirect command. The first Aurius mentioned is Aulus Aurius; the second Aurius is assumed by most to be Aulus Aurius Melinus (ex-husband of Cluentia and now husband of Sassia), whom Cicero later mentions was murdered by Oppianicus the Elder. Gaius is unlikely to be the son of Sassia, since Cicero does not mention him again. Sextus Vibius is given an explanatory relative clause by Cicero.

capitis periculum: This is a technical term for the particular charge for which Aulus Aurius would have prosecuted him: 'a capital charge'. *caput* means 'head' and therefore 'life', but it also refers to one's rights as a Roman citizen. Oppianicus the Elder would not have been killed if found guilty (it was highly unusual to kill a Roman citizen even on a capital charge), but rather exiled (so he would have lost his Roman citizenship).

ostentarat: = *ostentaverat*. An indicative because it is information being added by Cicero and therefore parenthetical and outside the grammar of the clauses.

quo: This is ablative after the verb **[dicebatur] esse usus**: 'whom [he was said] to have used as . . .'

sequestre: This is a term used especially in bribery. A *sequester* was the man who received the money from the briber and held it until the purpose of the bribe had been completed. The *sequester* would then release the bribe to the person for whom it was intended. Oppianicus the Elder wants Sextus Vibius dead so that no evidence of his misdeeds remains.

in illo indice corrumpendo: Another instance of gerundival attraction (see p. 50): 'in the corruption of that informer'.

dicebatur: Indicative, like **ostentarat** above.

proscribendos interficiendosque curaret: For *curo* and the gerund/gerundive, see p. 53. **proscribendos** and **interficiendos** are both masculine accusative plural because Oppianicus the Elder must see to the proscription and killing of four men. Notice the violence with which Oppianicus treats his enemies; he is not hesitant about killing.

proscribendos: Proscription was a technical term. *proscribere* literally means 'to write up'. A list would be published with the names of people whose property was to be confiscated or, in extreme cases like this, who were to be killed.

illis crudelissime interfectis: An ablative absolute. Notice the superlative adverb which creates greater pity for the victims of Oppianicus the Elder's proscriptions.

non mediocri . . . metu: **mediocri** is ablative agreeing with **metu**. Cicero uses litotes here to emphasize his point: 'by no modest fear', i.e. 'by great fear'.

ab eo: i.e. Oppianicus the Elder.

ceteri: This is nominative plural and refers to the citizens of Larinum: 'the other citizens'.

terrebantur: The passive of *terreo* gives a greater force to the fear felt by the citizens of Larinum.

in causa iudicioque: **in** would probably be best translated as 'during'. **causa** and **iudicio** are almost tautologous: 'during his court-case and trial'.

quis est qui: 'who is there who . . .?'

arbitraretur: This is a generic subjunctive. **qui** and a generic subjunctive mean 'the kind of person who would . . .' This question is probably best translated as something similar to 'who is there who could think . . .?'

5

haec: Neuter nominative plural referring to all the crimes of Oppianicus the Elder so far narrated. There are more to come.

cognoscite reliqua: **cognoscite** is a plural imperative addressed to the jurors. It is often used by Cicero to point out when he is putting forward a new argument or giving new evidence. **reliqua** is neuter accusative plural.

ut . . . miremini: A purpose clause dependent on **cognoscite**: 'know the remaining deeds so that . . .' **miremini** is second person plural and introduces an indirect statement: 'so that you may be amazed that . . .'

aliquando . . . aliquamdiu: 'finally . . . for any length of time'.

videte: Another imperative.

Sassiam in matrimonium ducere . . . concupivit: Oppianicus the Elder is the subject of the main verb **concupivit.** Sassia (the mother of Cluentius) is the object of **in matrimonium ducere** which is dependent on **concupivit. in matrimonium ducere** means 'to marry' and is used of a man marrying a woman.

Habiti matrem: Cicero here refers to Cluentius by his cognomen (his third name) rather than his nomen (his second name). Cicero emphasizes again the relationship of Sassia and Cluentius to draw attention to the unnatural way she has behaved in bringing him to trial.

illam: Repeated as in disbelief given the relative clause which Cicero provides.

cuius virum Aulum Aurium occiderat: **virum** here should be translated as 'husband'. From this statement, it seems to make sense that the **alterum Aurium** in the previous section is Sassia's husband (see p. 58).

utrum . . . an: 'whether . . . or'. This is an indirect question introduced by **difficile dictu est.**

utrum . . . nubat: This indirect question is missing a main verb; we must supply a verb such as *esset*. **hic** refers to Oppianicus the Elder and **illa** to Sassia; they could be translated as 'the former . . . the latter', but would be fine as just 'he . . . she'. **si nubat** is a remote future conditional: 'if she were to marry'.

dictu: This is an example of the supine. The supine is used in the dative/ablative (ending in -*u*) with certain adjectives to mean 'to X' (e.g. in the current example: **difficile dictu est** – 'it is difficult to say').

sed tamen: Used for emphatic reasons: 'But still . . .'

utriusque: Genitive of *uterque*: 'of each'. The reference is to Oppianicus the Elder and Sassia.

humanitatem constantiamque: *humanitas* is about their feelings and *constantia* about their deeds. These words are used with a large amount of irony.

petit: This verb is an example of the historic present (see p. 42) and it is promoted to the start of the sentence, accentuating it hugely. Oppianicus the Elder is the subject.

ut sibi Sassia nubat: Notice that Sassia is the subject of the indirect command, giving her agency.

magno opere: This phrase literally means 'with great labour'. The noun phrase effectively becomes an adverb: 'most earnestly'.

non admiratur audaciam: *admiror* has no sense of 'admire', but rather surprise and shock. Sassia is not astonished by his audacity.

admiratur . . . aspernatur . . . reformidat: Notice the historic presents.

non . . . non . . . non denique: An ascending tricolon with anaphora of **non**. 'Ascending' refers to the way in which the tricolon builds to a climax; notice the last phrase of the tricolon is longer and far more gruesome and explicit.

viri sui sanguine: i.e. the blood of Aulus Aurius Melinus, her former husband.

redundantem: This is a particularly evocative word and Cicero takes pains to give a sickening image of the house dripping with Aurius Melinus' blood. It is, of course, metaphorical.

quod . . . idcirco: 'because . . . for that reason'. **quod** introduces a subordinate clause in the indirect statement after **respondit**, which is why the verb **haberet** is subjunctive. However, Cicero wants to promote that clause as much as possible to show what a strange reason she had not to marry Oppianicus the Elder.

qui pecuniam Sassiae concupivisset: Cicero subtly suggests the real reason why Oppianicus the Elder wants to marry Sassia; it has nothing to do with her, rather her money. **concupivisset** is subjunctive because this is a causal **qui** clause: 'because/since/as he desired . . .'

domo ... moram: **existimavit** introduces an indirect statement here. **sibi quaerendum remedium** is a gerundive of obligation; the person who must do the action (the agent) is expressed in the dative case (**sibi**): 'a remedy was needing to be sought by him'. It is much more natural to make this active in English: 'he needed to seek a remedy'. **ad eam moram** expresses what the remedy is for: 'Oppianicus thought that he must seek a remedy to that delay . . .'

domo: *domus* takes the locative (see note on p. 54), therefore needs no preposition. Notice that it is ablative and therefore he is not seeking a remedy *in* his own home, but rather *from* his own home. It means that he does not have to seek far for a remedy to his having three children, as we shall see . . .

ex Novia infantem filium: This second son is mentioned here, but only to establish his whereabouts. The main story of this sentence is about **alter eius filius**.

Papia natus: **Papia** is ablative. **natus** + ablative = 'son of . . .' Papia had been the wife of Oppianicus the Elder's brother-in-law before she married Oppianicus the Elder.

Teani Apuli: The town is Teanum in Apulia. Cicero specifies here to differentiate it from Teanum Sidicinum in Campania. **Teani** is in the locative case: 'in Teanum'.

quod . . . passuum: A **mille passuum** (lit. 'a thousand paces') is a Roman mile. *abesse a(b)* is the usual way in Latin of giving the distance one place is from another. Teanum is 18 miles from Larinum (to the east).

educaretur: This is subjunctive because it is still part of the causal **cum** clause: 'but since his other son … was being brought up …'

arcessit subito: **arcessit** is an historic present and **subito** highlights the immediacy of Oppianicus the Elder's actions.

puerum: Notice how Cicero gives the names of neither of these two children, as if to emphasize in what little regard Oppianicus the Elder held them. He also emphasizes their youth.

quod: Connecting relative referring to the summoning of his son.

ludis publicis . . . festis diebus: Both are ablatives of time when. The *ludi publici* are public games (such as gladiatorial games) and *dies festi* are days of religious festivals.

nihil mali: **nihil** often takes the partitive genitive: 'nothing evil'.

mittit: Notice the historic present and the lack of an object.

Tarentum: Tarentum takes the locative (see note on p. 54).

cum simulasset: The 'pretence' of going to Tarentum is more about the fact that he was making a show of going to Tarentum; he probably did go, but only in order to divert the suspicion of others. **simulasset** introduces an indirect statement: **se proficisci**.

eo ipso die: Ablative of time at which: 'on that very day'.

cum . . . visus esset: Concessive **cum** clause with the pluperfect passive of *videre*: 'although . . . he had been seen'.

hora undecima: The Roman day (from sunrise to sunset) was divided into twelve equal hours. These would obviously vary in length depending on the season.

valens: The word suggests that the boy's death is certainly unexpected.

ante noctem mortuus: Notice the short clause to emphasize the suddenness of his death.

antequam luceret: The use of the subjunctive expresses the idea that this is not just a temporal statement. Cicero is making a point that the body was burned before it became light for a reason; there is some sort of causal relationship between this clause and the main clause. He must burn the body before anyone can inspect it.

combustus est: Cremation is the usual Roman practice for funerals.

maerorem matri: Notice the juxtaposition and alliteration to draw attention to the effect on Papia and to evoke our pity for her.

prius . . . quam: As is regular in Cicero, *priusquam* has been split into its component parts. Translate *priusquam* where the **quam** occurs in order to make sense of the sentence.

hominum ... familia: Cicero uses a chiastic structure here (genitive, nominative, nominative, prepositional phrase with similar meaning to genitive) to emphasize the terrible way through which Papia finds out about her son's death: she heard about it through the gossip of others rather than a member of Oppianicus the Elder's household.

uno tempore: Literally 'at the same moment' (ablative of time when). We could translate it more naturally as 'as soon as'.

sibi . . . ereptum: The two subjects of the indirect statement are **filium** and **munus**: she has been robbed of her son and her duty of performing the funeral rites. In Roman times, it was the woman's role to wash and prepare the body of the dead person for the funeral. *eripio* uses the dative case (**sibi**) to express from whom something is taken.

de integro: 'afresh', 'anew', 'again'.

iam sepulto filio: The **iam** ('already') emphasizes the cruelty of Oppianicus the Elder in having buried her son without her.

dies . . . necatur: An example of an inverted *cum* clause: the *cum* clause contains what is really the main sentence. This is used to highlight both parts of the sentence: the temporal clause becomes the main clause, highlighting the small amount of time; the main clause becomes a *cum* clause and is emphasized by its placement as the second clause. Notice the use of the historic present in the *cum* clause: **necatur**.

ille alter filius infans: i.e. the son of Novia.

laetanti . . . confirmato: This is an ablative absolute, not dative. The ablative absolute describes Sassia's feelings, not Oppianicus the Elder (made clear by positioning). She has a mind which is rejoicing and strengthened by excellent hope.

nec mirum: 'And no wonder'.

quae . . . videret: The subjunctive is used because this is a causal *qui* clause: 'because she saw . . .'

se . . . delenitam: An indirect statement introduced by **videret**. **delenitam** = *delenitam esse.*

nuptialibus donis: 'marriage gifts', i.e. a dowry. Notice the parallel word order with **filiorum funeribus** to accentuate the shocking 'gift' with which Sassia has been wooed.

quod: Translate as something like 'whereas'.

ceteri: This means people in general or the general population: 'most people'.

ita . . . duxit: The **quod** is contrasting opposites, although the sense of the opposites is rather convoluted. Cicero is implying that the majority of people are more desirous of money because they have children (in order to keep them living in a healthy and comfortable way), but Oppianicus the Elder found the murder of his children more pleasant (**iucundius**) because of his love of money (which he would gain through their deaths). **ducere** means 'to reckon, think' in this context, introducing an indirect statement: 'that man thought that losing children was more pleasant on account of money'. The infinitive (**amittere**) can act as a neuter noun in the nominative of accusative case (hence the neuter comparative **iucundius**).

6

sentio, iudices, vos pro vestra humanitate . . . : Cicero directly addresses the jurors in a rhetorical tour de force, forcing us to conclude with him that Oppianicus the Elder is a man guilty of the most heinous crimes. He draws a contrast between the jurors at the current trial and the jurors in Oppianicus the Elder's original trial and he perfectly balances his sentences to emphasize how abhorrent the jurors of the original trial must have found the crimes being recounted. Notice his repetition of words, the short, punchy nature of the clauses and the build up to the climax in his final question of this section, finishing on the all-important word **innocentem**. He also highlights the jurors' own sense of *humanitas*: the feelings of goodwill all people should feel towards their fellow humans.

breviter: Cicero subtly suggests that he has only given us a short version of the crimes of Oppianicus the Elder.

tandem: This has more force than just 'at last' in a question of this nature. Perhaps translate it as 'indeed' or 'tell me'.

quo . . . animo: An ablative. In English it might be best to supply the preposition 'in' which can sometimes be omitted in Latin: 'In what mindset do you think they were . . .?'

fuisse illos: **illos** refers to the jurors in the original case.

quibus . . . iudicandum: This is a relative clause referring to the **illos** Cicero has just mentioned. **quibus** is in the dative case because the gerundive of obligation is being used (**audiendum . . . iudicandum**): the person who is obligated to do something goes into the dative case (see p. 63). **his** is ablative plural and agrees with **rebus**: 'about these things'. 'Those men who not only had to hear about these things, but also had to make a judgement on them'.

vos auditis de eo: The **de eo** is repeated in the consecutive clauses, but the **vos auditis** is left out for the sake of brevity: 'You are hearing about that man . . .'

in quem: 'against whom'. Cicero is saying that the jurors are lucky enough not to have to be the jury on Oppianicus the Elder's trial.

qui . . . multavit: Both **naturae** and **legibus** are dative after the verb **satisfecit**: 'who has paid his debts both to nature and to the laws'; notice that Cicero now repeats both these nouns to show how Oppianicus the Elder has paid his debts. **multavit** has a technical legal sense of being punished with a fine. It is followed by the ablative to explain how the fine has been exacted: the laws punished Oppianicus the Elder with exile, nature punished him with death. Cicero suggests that Oppianicus the Elder deserved his death.

auditis . . . auditis . . . auditis: Cicero now repeats his verb from earlier and does so in a tricolon which builds to a climax, with the last clause being far longer than the previous two. Notice the anaphora as well.

cum ea . . . dicuntur: When a **cum** clause refers to present time, it usually takes an indicative, as it does here: **dicuntur**.

copiosissime . . . breviter . . . strictimque: Notice the contrast, using a superlative in the first instance. Cicero says that there are so many details one could go into about the crimes of Oppianicus the Elder, but he has only done so briefly and summarily.

illi: This refers to the jurors in the trial eight years prior to this one when Cluentius had prosecuted Oppianicus the Elder (see Introduction).

audiebant de eo: Again, Cicero introduces the verb (now in the imperfect tense) but does not repeat it in the subsequent clauses until we get to the tricolon at the end of his list, mirroring precisely the first half of this section through his use of **de eo**.

iurati: Perfect passive participle (in the masculine nominative plural) from *iuro*: 'to swear (an oath)'. The jurors would have been sworn in for their duty to act as an independent jury during the trial.

praesentis: Genitive of *praesens*, agreeing with **cuius**. Translate as 'standing before them' or 'face to face'. **cuius** is modifying **vultum**.

oderant: Cicero makes no pretence that the jury were impartial. How could anyone not hate such a monster?

cum . . . diceretur: Because this **cum** clause refers to the past, the subjunctive is usually used rather than the indicative (even though an indicative would have mirrored **cum . . . dicuntur** earlier even more).

Publio Cannutio, homine eloquentissimo: Publius Cannutius was Cluentius' lawyer in the trial between him and Oppianicus the Elder.

Publius Cannutius is mentioned elsewhere in Cicero's work as an excellent lawyer.

et est quisquam, qui: An indignant question: 'and is there anyone who . . .?'

Oppianicum . . . innocentem: This is an indirect statement introduced by **suspicari**. The infinitives are **oppressum** [*esse*] and **circumventum esse**. **circumventum esse** may carry its more figurative meaning of 'cheat' here.

innocentem: The word is given extra force by being the last one in its clause. It is clearly a sarcastic accentuation. The word is in apposition to **Oppianicum**: 'as an innocent man/although he was innocent'.

7

huius causae: **causae** is dative after **propiora**: 'nearer to the case'. **huius** is masculine genitive singular, referring to Cluentius: 'of this man'.

quaeso: This verb is often used in Latin to mean 'please'.

vos . . . memoria teneatis: **teneatis** is a jussive subjunctive (an 'order'): '(may you) hold'. **memoria** is ablative and, in English, we should supply the preposition 'in'. This phrase introduces an indirect statement.

non mihi hoc esse propositum: **hoc** is the subject of the indirect statement.

ut accusem Oppianicum mortuum: This purpose clause explains the **hoc** in the previous clause, which is not what Cicero set out to do in the trial. The **mortuum** emphasizes that it would be a fruitless task to prosecute Oppianicus the Elder.

cum hoc persuadere vobis velim: **velim** is the present subjunctive of the verb *volo* ('to want/be willing'). **persuadere** uses a dative for the person you wish to persuade (**vobis**) and an accusative for what you wish to persuade them of (**hoc**): 'Since I want to persuade you of this . . .'

iudicium . . . corruptum esse: This indirect statement explains the **hoc** in the previous clause. **ab hoc** refers to Cluentius.

uti: This infinitive is dependent on the earlier phrase **esse propositum**. Although previously Cicero used a purpose clause to explain what he had not set out to do, he now uses a simple infinitive to explain what he has set out to do. The variatio keeps the speech engaging and lively.

hoc . . . initio ac fundamento defensionis: Remember that *utor* is followed by an ablative case (**hoc**). **initio** and **fundamento** are in apposition to **hoc**: 'to use this as the beginning and foundation of my defence'. Notice that **hoc** has been used four times in this sentence – a very unusual occurrence.

Oppianicum . . . damnatum: Cicero's point in this rather long sentence is that he is giving the details of Oppianicus the Elder's crimes to show that he was guilty and that Cluentius did not bribe the jury; they made their decision based on facts and evidence.

qui: Connecting relative referring to Oppianicus the Elder.

uxori . . . dedisset: Cluentia, a previous wife of Oppianicus the Elder, is in the dative as the indirect object of **dedisset**. It is explained, through the relative clause, that she is the paternal aunt of Cluentius (not his sister mentioned earlier). The conjunction **cum** has been delayed.

subito: The main clause is introduced with excitement and shock. The explanation given in the main clause almost turns the **cum** clause into a causal clause: 'because he had given her . . .'

AS

illa: i.e. Cluentia.

se . . . mori: An indirect statement introduced by the verb **exclamavit**. Notice the use of the superlative **maximo** to describe her **dolore**, creating more pathos for her.

diutius . . . quam: **diutius** is the comparative form of *diu*. The English needs a little bit of reworking to make it make sense: 'And she lived no longer than she spoke'. The next sentence explains that she died whilst speaking. This may well be Cicero exaggerating the poisoning.

ad hanc mortem tam repentinam: **ad** here means 'in addition to'. Cicero tells us that, in addition to the suddenness of the death, everything else also points to poison.

in illius mortuae corpore: It is very common for possessive genitives to go in between the preposition and its noun (as here). **illius mortuae** refers to Cluentia: 'on the body of that dead woman'. Notice that Cicero uses polyptoton of the verb *morior* throughout this narrative of Cluentia's death to heighten the dramatic effect and to emphasize the cruelty of Oppianicus the Elder.

Gaium Oppianicum: The brother of Oppianicus the Elder.

in ipso fraterno parricidio: 'in the murder of his brother by itself'. What Cicero means is that you have to look no further than this murder to find every form of sin; but Oppianicus the Elder does go further. *parricidium* is most commonly the murder of a parent (specifically the father), though it can be used of the murder of any close relative, as here.

praetermissum: We must supply *esse* when we translate.

ut . . . accederet: A purpose clause dependent on the main clause: **aditum . . . munivit**.

aditum . . . munivit: *aditum munio* is a common phrase for road-building: 'to pave the way'. Cicero uses a metaphor to show that Oppianicus the Elder has been planning efficiently his crimes and laying down a path to reach his goal.

aliis sceleribus: Cicero is now going to tell us perhaps one of the most gruesome murders.

gravida Auria: This is the usual Latin word for 'pregnant'. Notice that Cicero uses the adjective before the noun, which is not the most common word order in Latin, to emphasize the horror of this murder. Presumably Auria is a relative of the Aurii whose family Oppianicus the Elder also tore apart with murder.

partus videretur: **partus** is the nominative singular and the subject of **videretur**: 'and since the birth now seemed to be approaching'.

post fratrem aggressus est: The **post** here explains the **ante** in the earlier clause. He kills Gaius' wife, Auria, before he kills Gaius (thus paving the way to this crime beforehand).

qui: This refers to Gaius Oppianicus.

exhausto illo poculo mortis: It is a fanciful touch to refer to the cup as *poculum mortis*: 'the cup of death'.

et de suo et de uxoris interitu: The **interitu** needs to be assumed after both prepositions: 'both about his own death and his wife's death'.

huius voluntatis: These words are in the genitive after **significatione**.

8–9: Cicero relates Oppianicus the Elder's dealings with a young man named Asuvius. Oppianicus the Elder ends up arranging the murder of Asuvius and the forging of his will in his own favour. When Asuvius' friends find his murdered corpse, they bring Oppianicus the Elder to trial under the judge Manlius. Manlius' dishonesty is

AS

notorious; Oppianicus the Elder bribes Manlius and is absolved of the crime.

10

quid?: Cicero uses this quite often to move forward his point: 'What about this?' 'Consider the following'.

aviam tuam, Oppianice: By promoting the object to the beginning of the sentence, Cicero emphasizes her. He also emphasizes her relationship with the current prosecutor, Oppianicus the Younger, by using **tuam** (and **tuus** later) and a vocative and adding **cui tu es heres** (see Section 3).

pater tuus non manifesto necavit: The rhetorical question is used to great effect to question the trustworthiness of Oppianicus the Younger given his father's actions.

medicum: This seems to be Oppianicus the Elder's personal doctor (**illum suum**). However, Cicero suggests that he works more as an assassin for him, emphasized by **saepe victorem**: 'often successful'.

mulier exclamat: Notice the historic present used for a vivid picture of the scene.

nullo modo: 'in no way'. This qualifies **velle**.

ab eo . . . quo curante: This describes the doctor. The relative clause is slightly odd because the relative pronoun (and its agreeing participle) form an ablative absolute: 'with whom giving care . . .' The best way to translate this into English is to avoid the participle and use a noun: 'under whose care . . .'

suos omnes perdidisset: The verb is subjunctive because it is in a subordinate clause within an indirect statement. The subject of the verb is Dinaea. **suos omnes** refers to 'all her children/relatives' (**suos** being used as a noun). This does not really match up with the narrative given in Section 3 and is probably hyperbole.

repente . . . aggreditur: Another historic present and the clause is introduced by **repente** to build up the dramatic nature of this story. The subject of **aggreditur** is Oppianicus the Elder and the verb here means 'approach', not 'attack'.

pharmacopolam circumforaneum: Lucius Clodius is a travelling drugs-salesman. Cicero's implication suggests that it is not the most respected career.

qui . . . venisset: The use of the subjunctive suggests a causal link: 'because he happened to be in Larinum at the time'.

duobus milibus HS: 2,000 sesterces. It is an ablative of price, telling us for how much the services of Lucius Clodius were bought. For **HS**, see note on p. 52.

id quod . . . demonstratum: This clause explains how Cicero knows the amount of money Oppianicus the Elder paid to Lucius Clodius. **ipsius** refers back to Oppianicus the Elder and is in the genitive: 'by his own tablets'.

cum eo . . . transigit: Another historic present: 'he does a deal with him'.

Lucius Clodius . . . confecit: A short, sharp sentence which deals with the matter quickly, just as Lucius Clodius did. He wasted no time, and nor does Cicero.

qui properaret, cui fora multa restarent: The subjunctives are used because these are causal **qui** clauses. Notice the asyndeton to keep the pace up. We can almost hear Lucius' own excuses complaining that he is in a hurry and has lots of country markets to visit.

sustulit: From *tollo*. Here it means 'he killed'.

Larini: The locative case: 'in Larinum'.

punctum . . . temporis: **punctum** is an accusative of time (how long) and **temporis** is the partitive genitive: 'for a moment of time'.

est . . . commoratus: This is the perfect tense of the deponent verb *commoror*.

eadem . . . faciente: An ablative absolute. We were told of Dinaea's death and the will in Section 3, but only now does it become clear that Oppianicus the Elder had a hand in it all.

qui gener eius fuisset: The subjunctive shows that this is causal and tells us how he managed to get his hands on the will. Notice that **fuisset** is pluperfect because Magia, Oppianicus the Elder's wife and the daughter of Dinaea, was dead by this point.

multis locis: We must supply the preposition 'in' in English.

eius: This refers to Dinaea: 'after her death'.

testamentum: This is the object of **obsignavit** and it has the perfect passive participle **transcriptum** agreeing with it.

signis adulterinis obsignavit: Oppianicus the Elder uses forgery to sign and seal the fake will so that no one will suspect.

multa praetereo consulto: 'I pass over many things deliberately'. Cicero cleverly hints at the many other crimes of Oppianicus the Elder without having to go into detail about them.

etenim vereor ne . . . : Cicero implies that the jurors are probably all suitably appalled by Oppianicus the Elder's behaviour that he does not need to talk about the number of other crimes he also committed.

haec ipsa: This is neuter nominative plural and the subject of **videantur**.

vos ... existimare debetis: Cicero brings the jury back into his speech by using the pronoun to strengthen the opening of this sentence. 'You ought to reckon ...' **existimare** introduces an indirect statement.

eum: This is Oppianicus the Elder who is the subject of the indirect statement.

similem sui: *similis* can take the genitive or dative. Cicero uses the genitive generally, but sometimes the dative with neuter nouns. **sui** is the genitive of the reflexive pronoun *se*: 'similar to himself'. In English we might say 'true to himself' or 'true to form'.

illum ... corrupisse: An indirect statement introduced by the main verb **iudicaverunt**. Oppianicus the Elder is the subject of the indirect statement (**illum**).

tabulas ... censorias: The official register of the censors kept in Larinum (each municipium would have its own public records maintained by its censors).

decuriones universi: The **decuriones** were the town council. They acted as the Senate of a municipium. **universi** here means that the town council judged this unanimously.

11

cum illo: This refers to Oppianicus the Elder.

rationem ... rem ullam: *ratio* has a wide variety of meanings, including 'calculation'; for this reason, it probably means 'financial dealings' here. **rem ullam** = 'anything'; the reference is probably to business transactions. Oppianicus the Elder has proven himself to be an untrustworthy individual.

contrahebat: The verb needs to be taken in both clauses within this sentence.

nemo illum . . . tutorem . . . liberis suis scripsit: A *tutor* was a legal guardian for children (and women). Women and children could only transact business deals through their *tutor*. The fact that no one wanted Oppianicus the Elder to be the legal guardian of his children again shows how he could not be trusted.

aditu . . . congressione . . . sermone . . . convivio dignum: *dignus* takes an ablative case, which explains the cases in this list of four nouns. **dignum** is in apposition to **illum**: 'no one judged him worthy of . . .'

ut . . . fugiebant: **ut** introduces a simile here (notice that the verb is indicative). **fugiebant** makes most sense if it is taken as the main verb of the simile rather than separately from it: 'as if they [all] were fleeing some huge . . . etc.' The comparison is hyperbolic, but serves to paint Oppianicus the Elder in the worst possible light.

audacem . . . nefarium . . . nocentem: These three adjectives are in apposition to **hunc hominem**, which of course refers to Oppianicus the Elder.

accusasset Habitus: In a past closed conditional, the pluperfect subjunctive is used in both halves of the sentence (**si . . . potuisset . . . accusasset**). The reversal of condition and consequence lends emphasis to this sentence: 'Habitus would *never* have brought him to trial if . . .'

salvo capite suo: This is an ablative absolute. Remember that *caput* often has a metaphorical meaning of 'life': 'with his life safe and sound.'

erat: The repetition almost has the effect of a concession on Cicero's part.

erat huic . . . attamen mater: A clever set of short clauses emphasizing the relationships of Oppianicus the Elder and Sassia with Cluentius. Cluentius has the decency to treat his mother and step-father in the manner he should, until his hand is forced by their indecency. Notice the repetition of **erat** at first and then its disappearance in the last two clauses.

remotum: We must supply *est* to complete the perfect passive *remotum est*. The subject is **nihil**: 'Nothing was [so] removed'.

quam Cluentius: Cluentius is compared with the **nihil**; we might have expected Cicero to use *nemo* seeing as he is talking about people becoming prosecutors, but the use of **nihil** produces a hyperbolic tone.

natura . . . voluntate . . . ratione: These nouns are in the ablative and they describe the character of Cluentius. Providing the preposition 'in' might make a better translation: 'in his nature, in his intention, in the way [of his life]'. Notice the tricolon.

cum esset . . . proposita: The subject of the sentence is **haec conditio** (a variant of *condicio*).

ut . . . : This introduces two purpose clauses (**aut accusaret, aut moreretur**), showing the ultimatum facing Cluentius. Cicero claims that prosecuting Oppianicus the Elder was a matter of life and death for Cluentius. Notice the parallelism in the two options open to Cluentius.

accusare . . . emori: Cluentius is forced into this decision; notice the chiasmus (**accusare quoquo modo . . . illo modo emori**) to emphasize and contrast the two verbs. *emorior* is a more emphatic version of *morior*.

12–25: Cicero relates Oppianicus the Elder's attempt on Cluentius' life (who was known not to have made a will). He attempted to poison Cluentius through an agent, Fabricius, who put his freedman, Scamander, on the case. Scamander asked Diogenes, the slave of Cluentius' doctor, to administer poison. However, Diogenes reported the plot to his master and Cluentius; Diogenes was asked to set a meeting with Scamander, and Scamander was caught red-handed with the poison. Cluentius tried Scamander and then Fabricius; both were convicted. He then brought Oppianicus the Elder to trial. After Scamander's and Fabricius' trials, Oppianicus the Elder could not escape conviction. However, he attempted to bribe the jury, using one of the jurors, Staienus, as his agent. Staienus plotted to keep the money for himself, and so the bribery attempt backfired, resulting in Oppianicus the Elder's conviction. Staienus was forced to pay back the money; Oppianicus the Elder went into exile.

26: Cicero proves that Cluentius did not poison Balbutius, through the testimony of Balbutius' father; this also absolves Cluentius of the attempted murder of Oppianicus the Younger.

27

unum . . . reliquum eiusmodi crimen est: Cicero marks his transition to the second part of his defence: the charge of poisoning Oppianicus the Elder. He hopes to answer this second charge in such a way as to leave no doubt for the jurors as to the innocence of Cluentius.

iudices: A direct address to the jurors, marking the transition even more clearly and strengthening the force of the second person plural verb **possitis**.

ex quo . . . possitis: **possitis** is subjunctive because this is a purpose clause introduced by the relative pronoun rather than *ut*: 'from which you may be able to . . .'

A Level

illud . . . quod: The relative clause after **quod** explains the **illud**.

dictum est: This phrase introduces an indirect statement of which the main clause is **id omne a matre esse conflatum**.

quidquid . . . quidquid: Notice the anaphora suggesting how many things Cluentius has suffered over the years. In both clauses, **quidquid** is the accusative and is followed (as is often the case) by a partitive genitive (or two): **mali** and **sollicitudinis ac negotii**. In English, we do not render the genitive: 'whatever evil . . . whatever worry and trouble'.

per hos annos: An emphatic phrase implying the long suffering of Cluentius; **per** is not strictly needed since the accusative of time, how long, would have produced the same meaning. The **per** is used for emphasis.

viderit . . . habeat: These two verbs are in the subjunctive because they are in a subordinate clause within an indirect statement. Notice the tenses: 'he has seen . . . he has'.

hoc tempore: Cicero contrasts this with all that Cluentius has suffered over the past eight years since the previous trial. Presumably the worry and trouble which Cluentius currently has is this very trial at which Cicero is speaking.

id omne: 'all that' referring to all the evil and trouble. This is the subject of the indirect statement.

a matre: True to his word earlier in the speech (see Section 1), Cicero refers to Sassia as Cluentius' mother to accentuate their relationship and therefore the cruelty of the woman.

esse conflatum: This is the perfect passive infinitive and it is the main verb of the indirect statement. The metaphor suggests a fire being stoked.

Oppianicum . . . dicitis: This whole sentence is an indirect statement introduced by the main verb (left until the end): **dicitis**. The subject of **dicitis** is the prosecution: 'you say'. Cicero uses the plural to include, presumably, the lawyer for the prosecution (Titus Accius), Oppianicus the Younger (the prosecutor) and Sassia (the puppet-master behind the scenes).

quod: This is a relative clause referring to the poison introduced in the last clause. **datum sit** is subjunctive because it is a subordinate clause within the indirect statement.

in pane: The poison was, apparently, administered through some bread. Cicero deals with the rather strange method of poisoning in Section 28.

per Marcum Asellium quendam: **per** here means 'through means of' or 'by'.

familiarem ipsius: **ipsius** refers to Oppianicus the Elder and is genitive: 'his own friend'.

in quo: This is a connecting relative: 'in this matter'.

illud: This hardly needs to be translated into English since it is explained by the following indirect question: 'In this matter, firstly I ask [this:] what reason was there . . .'

Habito: This is probably the dative of possession: 'what reason did Habitus have . . .'

cur: Fitting in 'why' to your English translation might be a little tricky if you want to have it continue to make sense. Perhaps it is best to translate it as 'as to why' or even just 'for': 'what reason did Habitus have for wanting . . .'

inimicitias: This word is in the accusative case and it is the subject of the indirect statement introduced by the main verb **confiteor**.

A Level

Notice the use of the plural to suggest how much enmity there was between the two men.

inter ipsos: Though strictly not grammatically correct (since any reflexive pronoun should refer back to the original speaker), the sense makes it clear enough that Cicero is talking about Cluentius and Oppianicus the Elder. This allows for extra emphasis through this word (although note that some editors use *eos* instead of **ipsos**).

confiteor: Cicero presents this as a grudging admission, even going so far as to use the plural in **inimicitias**. However, it is all part of his clever ploy because he is going to go on to prove that, if Cluentius did hate Oppianicus the Elder, he should have wanted his wretched life to be prolonged.

homines inimicos suos: Cicero uses **homines** to allow him to bring in a generalizing statement: 'people in general . . .'

morte affici: **morte** is the ablative of instrument: 'with/by death'. Notice that the infinitive is passive, taking out any suggestion of murder. Cicero is cleverly skirting round the charge of murder: 'people want their enemies to be punished with death . . .' There is no suggestion that normal people (like Cluentius) would actively seek to murder anyone, even if they did want their enemies to die.

aut . . . aut: The only two reasons which Cicero sees which could explain why someone might want their enemy dead.

quo tandem igitur . . . : The remainder of this section is an impressive display of Cicero's rhetorical power and force. Notice all the indirect questions building the idea of the ridiculous nature of the charge under which Cluentius is being prosecuted. Cicero points out the horrible life that Oppianicus the Elder was leading in exile and that Cluentius would not want to rob him of that humiliation and destitution by killing him. He ends the passage with a rhetorical description of the afterlife and the avenging spirits Oppianicus the Elder might face there. He claims that perhaps Cluentius, believing such 'stories', wanted to hasten Oppianicus the Elder's death. It is a fine example of persuasive oratory.

tandem: See note on p. 68.

quo . . . metu: **quo** is part of the interrogative pronoun and it agrees with **metu** (in the ablative of instrument): 'by what fear . . .?'

Habitus: This is Cluentius, referred to by his cognomen (third name) rather than his nomen (second name).

tantum in se facinus suscipere: **tantum** is neuter accusative singular and agrees with **facinus. in se suscipere** = 'to take up for himself' i.e. 'to undertake'.

quid erat quod . . . quisquam timeret: This is a rather complicated way of asking a question. Cicero is effectively asking 'why should anyone fear Oppianicus?' However he does so by using a relative clause which contains the main body of the question: 'what [reason] was there which [explains why] anyone should fear Oppianicus?'

eiectum e civitate: 'thrown out of the state' i.e. exiled. Oppianicus the Elder was found guilty in the trial eight years previous to this one and was therefore exiled (deprived of his rights as a citizen). See further in the Introduction.

ne . . . an ne . . . an ne: These are all fear clauses introduced by the question **quid metuebat**: 'What was he fearing? That . . .? Or that . . .? Or that . . .?' The anaphora has the effect of building up a contrast between the positions of Cluentius and Oppianicus the Elder.

perdito . . . condemnato . . . exsulis: These words all describe Oppianicus the Elder and point out how worthless his life was at the time of his death (which furthers Cicero's point about Cluentius wanting him to suffer as long as possible).

testimonio laederetur: Notice that Cicero reverses the word order (ablative then verb rather than in the previous two questions: **oppugnaretur a perdito** and **accusaretur a condemnato**) for a bit of variatio and to emphasize **exsulis testimonio.** As an exile, Oppianicus the Elder forfeited all the rights of a citizen, including taking part in any legal proceedings.

sin: 'but if'.

quod . . . idcirco: The causal clause introduced by **quod** is given repeated emphasis by **idcirco**: 'But if, because Habitus hated his enemy, for that reason he did not want . . .'

frui: This is the infinitive of *fruor* which takes an ablative case (**vita**).

adeone: This is *adeo* with *-ne* attached to introduce a question. Though not the first word of the sentence, *adeo* is the first word of the clause which contains the question itself and therefore *-ne* attaches itself to this word.

ut: A result clause introduced by **adeone erat stultus**: 'was he so stupid that . . . ?'

illam . . . arbitraretur: The main verb of the result clause is **arbitraretur** which introduces an indirect statement: 'that he thought that . . .' The subject of the indirect statement is **illam**: 'that one, which he (Oppianicus the Elder) was living at the time, was a 'life''.

damnati, exsulis, deserti ab omnibus: These three genitives qualify the **illam** from earlier: 'that (life) of a condemned man, of an exile, of a man deserted by everyone . . .' This explains why Cicero suggests it would be stupid to believe that such a life constituted 'living'.

A Level

quem: This is a relative clause referring to Oppianicus the Elder. It continues the explanation of why his life was so awful: 'The man whom no one . . .' The fact that the verb is in the subjunctive makes the *qui* clause causal and gives us the reason why he is **deserti ab omnibus**.

animi: A possessive genitive which is sandwiched between the preposition and its noun: 'on account of his insolence'.

nemo . . . nemo . . . nemo . . . nemo . . . vellet: The anaphora makes it clear that Oppianicus the Elder has been completely abandoned by everyone. The verb **vellet** must be taken with all the infinitives mentioned.

tecto: We must supply the preposition 'in' for our translation to make sense: 'in their house'.

huius: This is genitive and refers to Oppianicus the Elder.

vitae: This is dative after the verb **invidebat**: 'did he envy the life of this man?'

hunc: This is the accusative and the direct object of the verb *oderat*. It refers to Oppianicus the Elder.

acerbe et penitus: Notice the force of the two adverbs.

quam diutissime: **quam** + a superlative adjective or adverb = 'as X as possible'. Hence, **quam diutissime** = 'as long as possible'.

vivere velle debebat: Cicero has emphasized the terrible life Oppianicus the Elder lives to build up to this, his main point. If Cluentius really hated Oppianicus the Elder, it makes more sense that he would want him to live in such a state for as long as possible.

huic mortem: The **huic** is a dative of possession: 'his death'.

maturabat: The tense is important here: 'was an enemy hastening . . .' in effect means 'was an enemy likely to hasten . . .'

A Level

quod: Although this relative clause strictly describes **mortem**, the relative pronoun has become neuter (even though *mors* is feminine) to agree with **perfugium** which is in apposition to it: 'his death which was the only refuge . . .'

unum: The word *unus* can often mean 'only' as opposed to 'one' (although 'one' would also work: 'which was his one refuge . . .').

in malis . . . calamitatis: 'in the evils of his disaster'. Perhaps 'depths' would be a good translation for **malis** here.

qui: This is a relative clause which introduces a conditional clause; the relative clause explains the word **huic** later in the question: 'to a man who, if he had had [etc.], why would an enemy want to offer that which he ought . . .' It is a complicated sentence to render into English. It might be worth taking the main clause (**huic . . . deberet**) first and using the relative clause to explain the **huic** in the appropriate place.

si . . . habuisset . . . conscisset: The pluperfect subjunctive is used in both halves of the conditional clause: 'if he had had . . . he would have resolved upon . . .'

quid animi et virtutis: **quid** is used after **si** to mean 'any'; it is accusative here as the direct object of **habuisset** and is followed by two partitive genitives. **animi et virtutis** is an example of hendiadys (one through two) meaning 'any courageous spirit'.

ut . . . dolore: This parenthesis tells us that other brave men have chosen to kill themselves in Oppianicus the Elder's situation. This contrasts Oppianicus the Elder's courage with those of others. We need to supply a verb such as *habebat* to complete the sense: 'as many brave men often have had . . .'

mortem sibi ipse conscisset: *mortem sibi consciscere* is a technical term for committing suicide. Suicide in times of trouble was not seen as wrong by the Romans and, in fact, was seen as a brave act.

quamobrem: Originally separate words: *quam ob rem* – 'on account of what thing' i.e. 'why?'

vellet: This is a deliberative question, hence the use of the subjunctive: 'why would an enemy have wanted to . . . ?'

id . . . quod: **id** is the object of **offerre** and is explained by the relative clause introduced by **quod**.

quid . . . mali: A use of the partitive genitive: 'what (of) evil . . .'

nam . . . attulit: Notice the number of particles used in this sentence. Cicero points out that death has brought Oppianicus the Elder none of the evils which his life had provided him.

ineptiis ac fabulis: Ablatives of instrument: 'by the absurdities and stories'. Cicero implies that stories of the Underworld are foolish myths.

ducimur: First person plural present passive of *duco*: 'we are led'.

ut: This introduces a purpose clause: 'so that we . . .'

existimemus: This verb is in the subjunctive because it is in a purpose clause. It also introduces an extended indirect statement: **illum . . . regionem**.

apud inferos: The *(di) inferi* are 'the gods below' which is a euphemism for the Underworld.

impiorum supplicia: In Latin, a noun which is dependent on another noun tends to go into the genitive case. It is often better not translated as 'of' in English, though: 'punishments for wicked men'.

A Level

illic . . . hic: Cicero contrasts the enemies whom Oppianicus the Elder may have found in the Underworld with those he has left behind on the earth.

reliquisse: Technically this verb should be in the subjunctive because it is part of a subordinate clause within an indirect statement. However, it has been attracted into the infinitive to match **offendisse** and strengthen the comparison.

a . . . Poenis: The words **socrus**, **uxorum**, **fratris** and **liberum** are all in the genitive. **Poenis** is to be taken with all the prepositions and the genitives tell us to whom the *Poenae* belong. The *Poenae* are the avenging spirits, sometimes identified with the Erinyes (Furies) of Greek mythology. The repetition of the preposition and the length of the list reminds us how many murders Oppianicus the Elder has committed.

uxorum: Cicero has only insinuated that Oppianicus the Elder killed his first wife, Cluentia, not any of his others. However, the exaggeration is useful for reminding us how many enemies Oppianicus the Elder has.

actum esse: This is the infinitive of the indirect statement. The subject of the indirect statement is understood to be *illum* from the previous sentence: 'that he has been driven by . . .'

praecipitem: This adjective agrees with Oppianicus the Elder: 'headlong'.

in sceleratorum sedem atque regionem: **sceleratorum** is the genitive of possession placed between the preposition and its noun. **sedem atque regionem** is effectively hendiadys: 'to the place which is the home of the wicked'.

quae: A connecting relative in the neuter plural: 'these things'.

id quod omnes intellegunt: Cicero suggests that everyone understands that these stories of the Underworld are false. Clearly Cicero does not believe in the traditional view of the Underworld and he expects his jury not to believe. Cicero does, however, believe in life after death in some form given what he says in other works of his.

quid . . . aliud: 'What else . . . ?'

ei: This is dative after **eripuit** (i.e. 'from him') and it refers to Oppianicus the Elder.

quae . . . doloris: Cicero finishes his fine rhetoric by pointing out that, since the stories of punishment in the Underworld are false, death has taken nothing from Oppianicus the Elder except his ability to sense his pain. Therefore death is a relief from his troubles and Cluentius should not have wanted to hasten it for him. It is a logically sound argument; however, we are all aware that hatred and revenge do not always work in a logical way.

28

age vero: **age** is a very common interjection in Cicero: 'Well, come on now'.

datum: We must supply *est* to complete the sense of the sentence, turning *datum est* into a perfect passive.

per Marcum Asellium: Cicero answers his own rhetorical question. He has already mentioned that Marcus Asellius was the man who administered the poison, but he is going to emphasize the point now that Cluentius did not have a relationship with Marcus Asellius which would have been conducive to hiring him.

quid huic cum Habito: We must supply a verb like *erat* to complete the sense of this question. **huic** is the dative of advantage: 'What was

A
Level

there for him (i.e. Marcus Asellius) with Habitus?' In better English: 'What connection did he have with Habitus?' Cicero says that the answer is **nihil**: 'nothing'.

atque adeo . . . potius: 'no, further than that . . . rather . . .'

quod: A causal clause explaining why there was **simultas** between Cluentius and Marcus Asellius.

est usus: This verb can mean 'to be intimate with' or 'associate with'. It is still followed by the ablative.

potius etiam simultas: Again, we must supply the verb *erat*: 'rather there was even enmity'.

eine: *ei* + *-ne*.

eine . . . committebat: This sentence needs to be taken in sections:

- the main verb (of which Cluentius is the subject) is **committebat**;
- the objects of this verb are **et suum scelus et illius periculum**;
- **potissimum** needs to be taken with **ei** (the indirect object of the verb);
- finally, **quem** introduces a relative clause explaining **ei** (Marcus Asellius) which contains an indirect statement introduced by **sciebat**.

sibi offensiorem Oppianico familiarissimum: The **sibi** refers back to the subject of the main verb (i.e. Cluentius). The comparative **offensiorem** should be translated as 'rather hateful / overly offensive'. Marcus Asellius was offensive to Cluentius but very friendly with Oppianicus the Elder. Notice the comparative followed by the superlative to emphasize the nature of Marcus Asellius and Oppianicus the Elder's relationship.

eine . . . potissimum et suum scelus et illius periculum committebat: The tense of **committebat** is important again (as on p. 86): 'Was he likely to entrust . . . ?' The **scelus** refers to the apparent plot of Cluentius to poison Oppianicus the Elder and therefore the **illius periculum** is the 'danger to that man' (i.e. Oppianicus the Elder). Although **illius** is genitive, it is better translated as 'to that man' here. **potissimum** is an adverb and should be taken with **ei**: 'especially to a man whom . . .' Of course, the answer to the question is 'no' and therefore Cicero has proven the ridiculousness of the suggestion.

tu: This is addressed to Oppianicus the Younger.

qui pietate . . . excitatus es: *pietas* is the sense of duty to the gods, one's country and one's family. Cicero is giving the apparent motivation for Oppianicus the Younger's prosecution of Cluentius with more than a little irony.

ad accusandum: A gerund of purpose: 'to prosecute'.

inultum: Clearly Oppianicus the Younger bypassed the man who administered the poison and went straight for the prosecution of Cluentius as the brains behind the plot.

Habiti exemplo: Cluentius had tried the men who were to administer and arrange his poisoning before he tried Oppianicus the Elder eight years previously. (See Introduction for further details.)

ut . . . de hoc praeiudicaretur: This is a purpose clause. It is dependent on the previous clause: 'Why did you not use Habitus' example so that it might have been judged beforehand about this . . . ?' In English, it might be best to do away with 'so that' and just say 'and'. **praeiudicaretur** is an impersonal passive; in English we can turn it into an active verb: 'Why did you not use Habitus' example and have a judgement beforehand about this . . . ?' **de hoc** refers to the whole affair of the poisoning of Oppianicus the Elder.

per illum, qui attulisset venenum: The **per** introduces the way through which the matter might have been able to be judged

A Level

beforehand: 'through [the investigation of] that man who had administered the poison'.

iam vero: 'Well, now then . . .'

quam . . . quam . . . quam: The anaphora serves to delay the explanation of **illud** and build a sense of incredulity about the method through which the poison was supposedly given.

illud: We are missing a main verb such as *est*. It would be best in English to translate the **quam** clauses first and then *[est] illud*: 'how . . . how . . . how . . . that is, that . . .'

in pane datum venenum: An indirect statement explaining the **illud**; we must supply *esse* to make *datum esse* the perfect passive infinitive: 'that the poison was given in bread!' Cicero now goes on to show the absurdity of the suggestion that poison was administered in bread by asking lots of rhetorical questions highlighting the ridiculousness of it all.

faciliusne potuit quam: We must supply a verb such as *dari*: 'Was it able [to be given] more easily than . . .' Cicero probably does not include this verb because it can be understood from the previous sentence.

latius potuit abditum: Supply a verb such as *dissipari*: 'Was it able [to be dispersed] more widely having been hidden in . . .' The lack of an infinitive in this sentence has led some editors to question this passage and render it differently, some not treating this sentence and the next sentence as separate (allowing **permanare** to be the infinitive for both **latius potuit** and **celerius potuit**).

totum colliquefactum . . . esset: **totum** is being used adverbially: 'completely'.

celerius potuit: The final of three anaphoric rhetorical questions (though the next rhetorical question also starts with a comparative adverb, though it lacks *potuit*).

in venas . . . permanare: Notice the language which emphasizes the poison's journey through the veins and whole body. It is a rather gruesome image.

facilius fallere: Supply *potuit* (understood from all the previous questions). The fact that this question does not contain *potuit* produces the effect that Cicero has added the question on at the end, giving his speech variety.

si esset animadversum: 'if it had been noticed'. Cicero means: if the attempt had been noticed and an examination of the evidence occurred, would poison in bread or in a cup be more likely to avoid detection?

ita . . . ut: This is a result clause: 'in such a way . . . that'.

secerni: The passive infinitive of *secerno*: 'to separate, part, distinguish'.

at repentina morte periit: This is an imagined objection. Cicero creates an objection to his argument (one which he can obviously counter). Here the objection is that the speed of Oppianicus the Elder's death suggests that poison was used. **repentina morte** is an ablative of instrument.

quod: The connecting relative: 'this'.

si esset . . . factum . . . haberet: **factum esset** is a pluperfect subjunctive, whereas **haberet** is an imperfect subjunctive to emphasize that there would still, at this moment in time, be too little evidence to conclude poison: 'if this had happened . . . it would not have . . .'

ea res: This refers to the *repentina mors*: 'quick death'.

propter multorum eiusmodi mortem: 'on account of a death of this kind of many'. **multorum** is being used as a substantive and is in the genitive because it is dependent on another noun. In more natural English: 'on account of this kind of death in the case of many people'.

si esset suspiciosum ... pertineret: The exact same conditional structure as the previous sentence (above). The emphasis here suggests that (a) poison had not been suspected at the time of death and (b) even if it had been, it would not relate to Cluentius (even now at the time of this trial).

potius quam: 'rather than'.

in eo ipso: 'in that very affair' i.e. the story of Oppianicus the Elder's sudden death.

impudentissime mentiuntur: Notice the superlative adverb to accentuate the sense of shamelessness with which the prosecutors and their witnesses are conducting themselves. In Section 29, Cicero will explain 'the truth' of Oppianicus the Elder's death.

id: This belongs within the **ut** clause and is the object of **intellegatis**. It is also explained by the clause **et . . . quaesitum**.

ut intellegatis: A purpose clause after **cognoscite**: 'Learn now so that you may understand . . .'

mortem eius: **mortem** is in apposition to **id**; **eius** refers to Oppianicus the Elder: 'so that you may understand the matter, both his death and . . .'

quemadmodum ... quaesitum: **quemadmodum** (originally *quem ad modum*) = 'how'. This whole indirect question is in apposition to **id**. The main verb is **sit ... quaesitum** (subjunctive because it is in an indirect question). The subject of the clause is **crimen**.

in Habitum: 'against Habitus'.

a matre: Another reference to Sassia. Cicero will soon explain (in Sections 30–32 and 35–37) the ways in which she has tried to destroy her son.

29

undique exclusus: 'shut out on all sides'. This has the same force as **deserti ab omnibus** earlier, suggesting that no one would open their door to Oppianicus the Elder anymore.

in Falernum: This is being used substantively for *in Falernum agrum*. The Ager Falernus was a region in northern Campania famous for its wine.

in morbum incidit: A common expression in Latin for falling ill (literally 'he fell into illness').

satis vehementer diuque aegrotavit: Literally 'he was sufficiently violently sick and for a long time'. The **satis** does the job of emphasizing the **vehementer**. In English it might be best to change it into a noun phrase: 'he had a very violent and long sickness'.

una: This is an adverb meaning 'together with'. Sassia has accompanied her husband into exile.

Sexto Attio quodam: This is in the ablative after the verb **uteretur**. Sassia is the subject of **uteretur** and it should be translated as 'was associating with'. Sextus Attius is described by the words **colono, homine valenti** and the relative clause introduced by **qui**.

homine valenti: **valenti** is ablative case agreeing with **homine**. A participle will terminate in *-i* when it is being used purely as an adjective; the *-e* ending is for its use in participle phrases (like an ablative absolute). **homine valenti** = 'a healthy fellow / a fine figure of a man'.

A Level

simul: 'together' i.e. 'with her'.

familiarius ... quam: **familiarius** is a comparative adverb and the comparison is after **quam**: 'more intimately ... than ...'

vir dissolutissimus: 'a very negligent husband' i.e. Oppianicus the Elder. Even he could not bear her association with Sextus Attius.

incolumi fortuna: An ablative absolute which effectively is equivalent to a conditional clause: 'even if his fortune had been unharmed'. Cicero's point is that Sassia was associating more intimately with Sextus Attius than a very negligent husband could bear even if he had not suffered ill fate.

posset: This is subjunctive because it expresses action at the same time as **uteretur**.

Nicostratus ... : This is actually the main clause, since the previous sentence has all been governed by the causal **cum**. For that reason, it might be best to replace the semicolon in English with a comma to avoid an incomplete clause.

servulus: The diminutive in Latin can be used as either abuse or endearment, depending on the context. Here it is used to mean 'a favourite slave'.

percuriosus et minime mendax: 'highly inquisitive and not at all a liar'. Unfortunately for Nicostratus, this will come back to bite him after Oppianicus the Elder's death.

dicitur: It is common in Latin to use the passive of *dico* when reporting rumours: 'Nicostratus is said to ...' The infinitive we want after **dicitur** is not **renuntiare** but the perfect infinitive **solitus esse** (from the semi-deponent verb *soleo*): 'to have been accustomed to ...' Although *dico* introduces an indirect statement (therefore we might assume that an accusative and infinitive are needed: *se solitum esse*), because in the passive Nicostratus is the nominative, the infinitive must agree with him: *solitus esse*. **multa** is the subject of **renuntiare**.

diutius: The comparative of *diu*: 'for any longer'.

ferre: As well as meaning physically carrying something, this verb often has the metaphorical meaning 'to bear / endure'. The object is the **improbitatem coloni**.

huc ad urbem: *urbs* is quite often used on its own to refer to Rome. **huc ad urbem** must here mean 'here to the neighbourhood of Rome' since Oppianicus the Elder, as an exile, was not allowed to enter the city.

aliquid . . . conducti: **conducti** is a partitive genitive after **aliquid**: 'some sort of hired house'. The phrase highlights how down on his luck Oppianicus the Elder is: he has to hire lodgings outside the city itself.

dicitur: See note on p. 97. There are three infinitives dependent on **dicitur**: **cecidisse, offendisse** and **esse mortuus**.

homo infirma valetudine: This is in apposition to Oppianicus the Elder: 'a man in poor health'. This explains why the injury to his side was so serious: because he was already in ill health (notice that **convalesceret** earlier was in the imperfect, suggesting that his recovery was still ongoing).

latus: From *latus, lateris*, n.: 'side, flank'.

posteaquam: This introduces a subordinate clause in what is an indirect statement, hence the subjunctive **venerit**.

ad urbem: Again, 'to the neighbourhood of the city'. He still would not have been allowed into Rome.

cum febri: 'with a fever'.

mortis ratio: 'the manner of his death'.

aut . . . aut: 'either . . . or'.

nihil . . . suspicionis: **nihil** is followed by the partitive genitive (as is often the case): 'no suspicion at all'. The subject of **habeat** is **ratio**.

id . . . versetur: **id** is the subject of the deponent verb *versor*: 'it is situated . . .'

in domestico scelere: Cicero says that it seems highly unlikely that Oppianicus the Elder was murdered, but if he was, then it was carried out by someone close to home. Is this a subtle accusation of Sassia?

30

nefaria mulier: In apposition to Sassia: 'Sassia, that abominable woman . . .'

filio: Dative of disadvantage: 'for her son'.

quaestionem: A *quaestio* is a judicial inquiry or investigation of some sort. Cicero suggests that the inquiry into the death of Oppianicus the Elder was nothing more than Sassia's desperation to destroy her son.

de Aulo Rupilio: 'from Aulus Rupilius'. **de** is the usual preposition when buying from someone in Latin.

quo . . . medico: The main verb is **erat usus**, the pluperfect of *utor*. **medico** is in apposition to **quo** and both are in the ablative after **erat usus**: 'whom Oppianicus had used as a doctor'.

Stratonem quendam: Strato is the object of **emit**; he is a slave.

quasi ut idem faceret: 'as if to do the same thing . . .' **ut** introduces a purpose clause and **idem** is explained by the following relative clause.

quod . . . fecerat: See Introduction (p. 9) for the context of this.

de . . . de: Sassia claims that she is looking into the conduct of Strato and one of her own slaves, Ascla.

quaesituram esse dixit: An indirect statement with the reflexive pronoun (*se*) omitted. This can be explained by the fact that the future active infinitive uses the future participle (**quaesituram**) and therefore the information on gender can be gleaned from this: 'she said that she would make an inquiry about . . .' In Rome, a slave was only allowed to give evidence under torture.

servum illum Nicostratum: Nicostratus (see Section 29) passed into the possession of Oppianicus the Younger after the death of his father. Nicostratus is the object of **postulavit** and the relative clause **quem . . . arbitrabatur** gives us more information about him.

quem . . . arbitrabatur: The main verb of this relative clause is **arbitrabatur** which has Sassia as its subject and introduces an indirect statement.

nimium loquacem: See the note on p. 97.

ab hoc adulescente Oppianico: *a(b)* after *postulo* means 'to demand [something] from . . .' Sassia asks Oppianicus the Younger to give her Nicostratus **in quaestionem**: 'for questioning' (i.e. torture).

puer: Oppianicus the Younger would have been around eighteen at this point. Cicero is probably emphasizing his youth to show that Sassia was taking advantage of him.

de patris sui morte: **patris sui** is a possessive genitive sandwiched between the preposition and the noun: 'about his father's death'.

constitui diceretur: The passive of *dico* is used again: '[since that inquiry] was said to be established about . . .'

etsi: 'although'. The main verb of this concessive clause is **arbitrabatur** (Oppianicus the Younger is the subject) and it introduces an indirect statement: **illum servum . . . fuisse**.

et sibi . . . et patri: 'both to him . . . and to his father'. **sibi** refers back to the subject of the main verb (i.e. Oppianicus the Younger).

benevolum: Cicero builds some pathos for Nicostratus, who had been a devoted slave but could not be saved from Sassia's evil intentions.

esse . . . fuisse: Notice the use of the two tenses of the infinitive. Because Oppianicus the Elder is now dead, the perfect infinitive **fuisse** is used ('had been'), whereas the present infinitive is used with Oppianicus the Younger because he was still his slave at the time ('was'). Keep this distinction in your English translation: 'although he thought that he was devoted to him and had been devoted to his father . . .'

nihil . . . recusare: After some lengthy subordinate clauses, we reach our main clause: Oppianicus the Younger does not dare to refuse his step-mother's request.

advocantur: An example of the historic present. The verb is also given extra emphasis by being at the beginning of its clause.

amici . . . ornati: The many friends and guests of Oppianicus the Elder and Sassia are described in very positive terms by Cicero. This is rather a surprise given all that Cicero has said about Oppianicus the Elder and Sassia: how do they have any friends who could be described as 'distinguished and eminent in all things'? Cicero presumably sets it up this way to show how out of order Sassia's behaviour is when one of her friends objects (in Section 31).

tormentis omnibus vehementissimis: Notice the emphasis on how horrific the torture is by the use of **omnibus** and a superlative: 'with all the most violent torture methods'.

quaeritur: An impersonal passive: 'it was investigated'. We would probably say more naturally in English: 'they (i.e. the slaves) were tortured . . .' Notice the historic present.

essent . . . tentati: The pluperfect passive subjunctive of *tento* (=*tempto*).

tamen: 'still . . .'

ut arbitror: A parenthetical aside to show us that this is Cicero's conjecture. It once again emphasizes the honest character of those who have been summoned.

auctoritate advocatorum adducti: **adducti** is a perfect passive participle in the nominative masculine plural describing the slaves. **auctoritate** is an ablative of instrument: 'having been led by the moral support of those who had been called'. The upright nature of those who had been called allowed the slaves to stick to the truth.

in veritate manserunt: 'they remained in truth' i.e. 'they stuck to the truth'.

neque . . . dixerunt: It is most common to find a negative indirect statement introduced by *nego* ('to deny') rather than *dico* and *non*. However, the use of this construction shifts the emphasis of the negative to the infinitive of the indirect statement: 'they said that they did not know anything'.

31

illo die: The first day of the inquiry is called to an end **de amicorum sententia**: 'by the judgement of her friends'.

satis longo intervallo post: = *post satis longum intervallum*: 'after a long enough interval'.

A Level

advocantur ... habetur ... praetermittitur: Three more historic presents, bringing the actions of the investigation vividly in front of our eyes.

de integro: See p. 66.

nulla vis tormentorum acerrimorum praetermittitur: Cicero emphasizes once again the true viciousness of the torture. Apparently, no method of the fiercest torture was left out of the proceedings.

aversari . . . posse . . . furere: This are examples of historic infinitives. The historic infinitive is a construction in Latin where a past main verb is replaced by a present infinitive. We cannot represent it in English and must translate them as if they were imperfect tenses. The effect of the historic infinitive is to draw attention to the *action* of the verb rather than the tense (an infinitive is effectively treated as a verbal noun in Latin).

sibi . . . procedere: This is an indirect statement dependent on **furere**: 'she was raging that . . .' **ea** is neuter accusative plural and the subject of the indirect statement; it is further explained by the relative clause **quae cogitasset**: 'those things which she had planned . . .'

ut sperasset: **sperasset** is syncopated. Although the verb is in the subjunctive, this is only because it is a subordinate clause within an indirect statement; the corresponding direct statement would be *ut speraverat*: 'as she had hoped'.

essent . . . defessa: Although the adjective describes both the **tortor** and the **tormenta**, it has been attracted into the neuter plural by its proximity to **tormenta**. Cicero is no doubt being hyperbolic here, suggesting that even the torture devices are worn out.

neque tamen: 'and yet . . .' This is still part of the **cum** clause: 'and yet she was not willing . . .'

illa: i.e. Sassia.

quidam ex advocatis: 'one of those who had been called'. **homo . . . praeditus** is in apposition to this.

aliquid falsi: **falsi** is a partitive genitive after **aliquid**.

hoc: The statement made by the man in the previous sentence.

ex omnium sententia: 'from everyone's opinion' i.e. 'unanimously'.

constitutum est satis videri esse quaesitum: 'it was decided that it seemed to have been investigated enough'. The **videri** represents the words used by those who were witnessing this.

redditur . . . proficiscitur: More examples of the historic present.

Larinum: The investigation actually took place in Rome (see section 184 in the English).

ipsa: i.e. Sassia. **cum suis** refers to her entourage.

quod: Cicero makes it clear that Sassia is not grieving because of the loss of her husband or because the true details of his death were not found out, but rather because her son would be unharmed. Another example of her lack of motherly affection for Cluentius.

fore: = *futurum esse.*

ad quem . . . perveniret: This is a relative clause referring to Cluentius. The **ad** should not be translated in English; it is only there because the verb *pervenio* so often uses *ad*: 'to arrive at'. Here, **perveniret** is best translated as 'reached' so the **ad** becomes superfluous in English. The verb is in the subjunctive because it is a subordinate clause within an indirect statement.

non modo . . . sed ne . . . quidem: Technically there should be a second *non* after **non modo** to negate the first clause: 'whom not only

A
Level

did *no* true charge reach, but not even a false suspicion'. However, these sentences are very common and the negative is often omitted if the sense is clear.

cui: Another relative clause referring to Cluentius. **cui** is in the dative after the verb **nocere**: 'whom . . . [the plot] had not been able to harm'. **potuissent** is in the subjunctive because we are still within the indirect statement.

non modo . . . sed ne . . . quidem: See note above. Notice the identical sentence structure.

aperta inimicorum oppugnatio . . . occultae . . . matris insidiae: Notice the parallelism to strengthen the contrast between 'his enemies' open attack' (i.e. the poisoning) and 'his mother's hidden plot' (i.e. to blame Oppianicus the Elder's death on him).

quae . . . simulasset: **quae** refers to Sassia. Because the verb is subjunctive, the relative clause is not a simple relative clause; here it is concessive: 'although she had pretended that . . .' **simulasset** introduces an indirect statement.

sibi persuasum esse: This is the impersonal passive: 'that she had been persuaded that . . .'

ei . . . tabernam dedit: The **ei** refers to Strato. Sassia is the subject of **dedit**. Sassia rewards Strato despite the fact that she accused him of apparently poisoning her husband. The contradiction here is supposed to raise suspicion about Sassia's motives.

instructam . . . et ornatam: These two adjectives describe the shop which Sassia has given to Strato: 'furnished and stocked'.

Larini: The locative.

medicinae exercendae causa: **causa** can be used with a gerund or gerundive to express purpose: 'for the sake of practising medicine'.

Strato had been the slave of a doctor and so presumably knew a little about the trade. Sassia will regret her generosity towards Strato (see Section 32).

32

unum, alterum, tertium annum: Accusatives of time how long: 'for one year, then another, then a third ...' Notice that Cicero presents Sassia as biding her time and seething through all three years.

ut ... videretur: A result clause: 'with the result that she seemed ...'

velle atque optare ... potius quam ... struere et moliri: Sassia seems to be 'wanting and wishing' some calamity on her son rather than 'contriving and working upon' it. The contrast is cunning: **velle** and **optare** are passive acts whereas **struere** and **moliri** are active ones. She still hates her son, but she is not actively doing anything about it currently.

Hortensio et Quinto Metello consulibus: An ablative absolute. It is common for Romans to use the names of the consuls to identify the year. Quintus Hortensius and Quintus Metellus were the consuls in 69 BC. **et** is not printed in other versions of the text.

ut ... detraheret: A purpose clause explaining Sassia's actions in the main clause (**despondit** ... etc.). *detraho* means 'to remove' and here has the meaning of removing Oppianicus the Younger from the other matters which require his attention and **ad hanc accusationem**.

aliud agentem: This describes Oppianicus the Younger: 'doing something else'. Cicero means that he has his mind now on other things and is quite indifferent to the prosecution of Cluentius.

despondit: *despondo* ('to betroth, promise in marriage') takes an accusative (the person promised: **filiam suam**) and a dative (the person to whom they are promised: **invito ei**).

A Level

invito ... ei: **ei** refers to Oppianicus the Younger. Cicero describes him as *invitus* ('unwilling') but yet again he cannot go against the wishes of his step-mother.

illam quam ex genero susceperat: This relative clause makes it clear that it is not Cluentia (Cluentius' sister) who is betrothed to Oppianicus the Younger, but rather Auria, Sassia's daughter by Aulus Aurius Melinus (who had once been her *gener* – 'son-in-law'). *suscipio* has a technical meaning of acknowledging a child (originating from the act of taking the child into one's arms). We can translate as 'she had conceived by ...'

ut: Another purpose clause explaining further the reasons why Sassia betrothed Auria to Oppianicus the Younger.

eum ... posset habere in potestate: 'so that she could have him in her power'. Sassia hopes that the marriage and, therefore, the hope of inheritance will force Oppianicus the Younger to do her bidding. **alligatum** and **devinctum**, with their very similar meanings, both describe **eum** (i.e. Oppianicus the Younger) and are attended by ablatives of instrument: **nuptiis** and **spe**.

Strato ille medicus: 'Dr Strato'. Cicero is using this term sarcastically given the story he is going to unfold.

domi: The locative case: 'at her house'.

furtum ... et caedem eiusmodi: The objects of **fecit**: 'he committed theft and murder of this kind'.

in aedibus: *aedes* in the plural tends to mean a house.

in quo sciret: The use of the subjunctive in this relative clause seems to indicate that the action of this verb is at the same time as the main verb of the **cum** clause (i.e. **esset**).

nummorum . . . auri: These are partitive genitives after **aliquantum**. A *nummus* is generally any denomination of coin and, therefore, in the plural is often a substantive for money.

noctu: An archaic form of *nox* which is often used as an ablative of time when or during (instead of *nocte*): 'at night'.

in piscinamque: The *-que* needs to be translated before the **in** if the sentence is to make sense. *-que* commonly attaches itself to the noun rather than the preposition.

armarii fundum exsecuit: Cicero will tell us how he managed to cut out the bottom of the chest shortly.

HS***: The actual amount is missing in the manuscripts. For **HS** (= 'sesterces') see the note on p. 52.

auri quinque pondo: We must supply *libras* ('pounds'). Originally **pondo** was an irregular ablative of *pondus, ponderis* n.: 'weight'. Hence, *auri quinque libras pondo*: 'five pounds of gold by weight'. Eventually the *libras* dropped out of the expression and **pondo** came to be treated as an indeclinable noun: **auri quinque pondo** = 'five pounds of gold in weight'.

uno . . . conscio: An ablative absolute: 'with one of the slaves . . . as his accomplice'. **puero non grandi** describes this slave.

furto postridie cognito: Another ablative absolute: 'with the robbery having been discovered on the next day'.

in eos servos: 'against those slaves'. Because the two slaves whom Strato had killed were not present, suspicion naturally fell on them.

comparebant: This is from *compareo* not *comparo*.

quaerebant homines: **homines** is masculine nominative plural and the subject of **quaerebant**: 'people were asking . . .'

A Level

quonam modo: **quonam** is from *quisnam* ('who on earth?') and is in the ablative to agree with **modo**: 'how on earth' (*quo* + *modo* = *quomodo* – 'in what way, how?').

recordatus est: This is the perfect tense of the deponent verb *recordor*. It introduces an indirect statement: **se ... vidisse**. **vidisse** itself introduces another indirect statement.

in auctione quadam: An *auctio* is a public sale at which the price of items increases (*augeo*) with the bidding. From this word is derived our English word 'auction'.

in rebus minutis: 'among the small things' i.e. 'among the odds and ends'.

aduncam ... serrulam: An indirect statement of which **serrulam** ('a small saw') is the subject and **venire** (from *veneo* ('to be on sale') not *venio*) is the verb.

aduncam ex omni parte dentatam et tortuosam ... serrulam: This is a very curious little tool. It is no wonder, given its rather strange description, that Sassia's friend recalled seeing it at the auction and that it becomes such a damning piece of evidence. It seems to be some sort of brace. We might like to translate this phrase as: 'a sort of small circular saw with hooked teeth all around and a crooked handle'.

qua ... videretur: A relative clause referring to the saw. The verb is in the subjunctive because it is a subordinate clause within an indirect statement. **qua** is an ablative of instrument. The subject is actually **illud** (referring to the **armarium**): 'by which that [chest] seemed to have been able to be sawed all around in this way'.

ne multa: 'No more'. This is equivalent to 'to cut a long story short'.

perquiritur ... invenitur: Note the historic presents and the promotion of the verbs to the beginning of their clauses to inject a bit

A Level

of excitement into the story (after a rather lengthy description of a saw . . .). **perquiritur** is an impersonal passive: 'an inquiry was made'. **invenitur** has a grammatical subject (**ea serrula**): 'that very saw was found . . .'.

a coactoribus: These are the men employed to go around after the auction and collect the money from those who had made purchases. **a** here means 'from' rather than 'by'; the *coactores* are being asked about who purchased the saw: 'an inquiry was made of the money-collectors'.

rem omnem dominae indicavit: 'he revealed the whole business to his mistress' i.e. 'he confessed everything to his mistress'.

homines: The two slaves killed by Strato.

in vincula: 'into chains' i.e. he was arrested.

etiam in taberna eius: The evidence against Strato is rather damning.

nummi, nequaquam omnes, reperiuntur: The verb is an example of the historic present. **nummi** is the subject of **reperiuntur**. **nequaquam omnes** is parenthetical explaining that they did not find all the money.

33–34: Cicero tells the jury that an inquiry into the burglary was held and Strato and Nicostratus were put to the torture once more. The inquiry was to deal with the burglary, but Strato's testimony does not even mention it (showing the stupidity of Sassia's forgery), but is wholly focussed on the alleged poisoning of Oppianicus the Elder.

35

videtis . . . iudices: Cicero addresses the jury now.

illam nefariam mulierem: The subject of the indirect statement. Once again, Cicero lets loose his vitriol on the woman.

A Level

qua, si detur potestas, interficere filium cupiat: This relative clause refers to **eadem manu. detur** is third person present passive subjunctive of *do*: 'with which, if the power were granted, she would want to kill her son'. Notice the use of **filium** to emphasize their relationship and therefore the shock of the juxtaposition: **interficere filium**.

hanc fictam quaestionem conscripsisse: *conscribo* means 'to compose' and here refers to the forgery of which Cicero has accused Sassia. **fictam** reinforces this: 'she has forged this false record of the investigation'.

dicite: 'tell me'. This is nominally addressed to the prosecution; however it comes across as an exasperated criticism of the lack of evidence. **dicite** introduces an indirect question: *dicite quis istam ipsam quaestionem obsignarit.*

unum aliquem: Cicero's tone becomes more accusatory as he continues to press home the point that the statement of Strato is clearly a complete forgery – and not even a very good one.

eiusmodi hominem: This refers to Sextus Attius (the farmer) who is referred to by Cicero as being present at the torturing of Strato (see section 182 of the English).

quem . . . nominari: In this relative clause, Cicero makes the point that he would prefer to have Sextus Attius as a witness than to have no one named at all. The suggestion is that Sassia could not even get an untrustworthy country bumpkin to sign her forged documents. **malim** is a potential subjunctive: 'whom I should prefer to be brought forth rather than no one to be named . . .'

quid ais, Tite Acci: An indignant question: 'What do you have to say for yourself, Titus Accius?' Cicero is shocked by the audacity of the prosecution for bringing a capital charge against Cluentius based on such flimsy evidence.

tu . . . afferes: Notice the anaphora and the tricolon building up to a climax. The whole sentence should be taken as a question (the question mark is in the next clause): 'Will you bring into the courtroom . . . ?'

periculum capitis: See note on p. 58.

indicium sceleris: 'proof of a crime'.

fortunas alterius litteris conscriptas: 'the fortunes of another (**alterius**) having been written in letters'. **litteris conscriptas** effectively just means 'in writing' or 'in a document': 'a document involving another man's fortunes'.

neque . . . neque . . . neque: Another tricolon. This second question explains why the first is so shocking. The prosecution is willing to provide evidence which could end with a man being charged with a capital crime and yet they will not name the author, signatory or witness of the evidence. Cicero feels that this is an insult to the seriousness of the trial.

neque . . . nominabis: 'will you not name . . . ?'

quam . . . hanc: The antecedent (**pestem**) of the relative clause has been attracted within it, which is a common phenomenon in Latin. The **hanc** then stands in for the **pestem** in the main clause. In English, we need to translate the **pestem** with the **hanc** rather than in the relative clause.

quam . . . deprompseris: **deprompseris** is a perfect subjunctive because this is a generic *qui* clause. Cicero is asking whether the judges will approve of 'this destruction, the kind which you have drawn out'. In English, the shorter phrase 'this kind of destruction which . . .' probably works better.

innocentissimo filio: 'for her most innocent son'. Notice the force of the superlative to suggest Cluentius' total innocence as opposed to the terrible crimes of the prosecution.

A Level

ex matris sinu: 'from the breast of his mother'. Once again, Cicero's insistence on pointing out the relationship between Cluentius and Sassia comes forth. This time he uses his imagery to show that Sassia has subverted the natural order of their relationship: a mother's breast is supposed to provide life to her children, not **pestem**.

hi tales viri: 'these men of such a kind' i.e. 'these honourable members of the court'.

esto: Third person singular imperative of the verb *esse*: 'let it be'. It is dismissive and suggests that Cicero does not even consider the document worth considering. A good English translation might be: 'But enough!'

in tabellis nihil est auctoritatis: **nihil** is followed by a partitive genitive: 'there is no authority in these documents'. Cicero dismisses the evidence put forward by the prosecution in a damning statement.

istis hominibus: These words are in the ablative case (we can tell this from **Stratone** which is in apposition to them). This is a use of the instrumental ablative with the verb *facere*: 'to do [something] with somebody'. Hence, **quid istis hominibus factum est**: 'What was done with those men?' or 'What became of those men?'

Stratone et Nicostrato: These two are in apposition to the **istis hominibus**: it is the fate of Strato and Nicostratus that Cicero wants to reveal now.

quaero abs te: **quaero** is often used with the preposition *a(b)* (**abs** is a common form) to specify of whom one is making their inquiry: 'I ask you ...' This introduces an indirect question, although the question word has been slightly delayed (**quid**).

Oppianice: A direct address to Oppianicus the Younger, the owner of Nicostratus (see Section 30 for their relationship).

servo . . . dicas: This phrase is an indirect question introduced by **quaero abs te**. The **quid** has been displaced slightly. Translate it as if it read *quid dicas factum esse servo tuo Nicostrato*. The **dicas** introduces an indirect statement; there is no accusative expressed because the **quid** serves the job of being the subject of the indirect statement: 'what you say was done with your slave Nicostratus'. **servo tuo Nicostrato** is ablative (see note on **istis hominibus**).

quem: A connecting relative referring to Nicostratus. Translate it as 'him'; he is the object of all the infinitives in this sentence.

tu . . . deducere . . . dare . . . servare . . . servare . . . servare . . . debuisti: The main verb is **debuisti** and Cicero includes the subject **tu** to make this an emphatic accusation against Oppianicus the Younger. The infinitives in this lengthy sentence are all dependent on **debuisti** and so, in our translation, we must translate **tu debuisti** first. Notice that the final three form a tricolon of **servare** making a subtle hint at what has happened to Nicostratus (made more poignant by Cicero's revelation of what has happened to Strato).

Romam: = 'to Rome' (see note on p. 54).

potestatem indicandi: 'the power of pointing out' i.e. 'the opportunity to give evidence'. **indicandi** is the genitive of the gerund.

incolumem: This agrees with Nicostratus and must be taken with all the instances of **servare**: 'to keep him unharmed . . .'

denique: Cicero's main point comes to light: where is Nicostratus now and why has he not been brought before the court to give his testimony?

quaestioni . . . his iudicibus . . . huic tempori: These are all datives of advantage: 'You ought to have kept him unharmed *for* this trial . . . etc'.

A Level

scitote: This is the second person plural (so-called) future imperative. Cicero uses it here for grand effect since it is rare and usually only used in legal documents: 'gentlemen of the jury (**iudices**), I have to inform you (**scitote**) that Strato's tongue was cut out (**exsecta lingua**) and he was crucified (**in crucem esse actum**)'. **scitote** introduces an indirect statement (hence the infinitive *actum esse*).

in crucem esse actum: *in crucem agere* literally means 'to drive onto the cross' and, therefore, 'to crucify'.

exsecta ... lingua: This action was presumably done before the action of **in crucem esse actum** and we can translate them as two separate main verbs (see note above on **scitote**). Strato's rather gruesome end is highlighted by Cicero to show that Sassia's evidence is lacking, and she knows it. Why else would she have to silence all her 'witnesses'?

quod: A connecting relative: 'this'. It is the object of **nesciat**.

nemo est Larinatium: **Larinatium** is genitive plural after **nemo**: 'there is not one of the citizens of Larinum ...'

qui nesciat: An indirect question introduced by the main clause (hence the subjunctive **nesciat**): 'who does not know [this]'. Cicero brings in anecdotal evidence to support his claim by saying that everyone in Larinum knows that Strato was killed. Notice the litotes: 'There is no one who does not know' = 'Everyone knows'.

timuit mulier amens: Notice the promotion of the verb lending it emphasis. Cicero also describes Sassia now as **amens** to highlight the insanity of what she has done.

non ... non ... non: A tricolon of things which Sassia *should* have feared, according to Cicero, emphasizing how **amens** she was to fear something else instead. Notice that the tricolon builds in its effect:

suam (affecting only Sassia) . . . **municipum** (affecting the people of Larinum) . . . **omnium** (affecting everyone – clearly hyperbole).

quasi . . . futuri: **essent futuri** is another example of the 'future in the past' (using the future participle of the verb *esse*): 'they were going to be'. **quasi** suggests that the whole clause is ridiculous: 'as if everyone was not going to be a witness to her crime'. Again, the litotes implies that everyone now knows about her wicked deed, despite the fact that she thought she could cover it up by killing Strato.

sic metuit ne: This answers the **timuit** from the previous sentence; notice the variatio to keep the speech engaging: 'She was afraid not of . . . but her one fear was that . . .' **ne** means 'that' in a fear clause.

extrema . . . voce: An ablative of instrument. **extrema** refers to the 'final' words of the dying man. *vox* is often used where the translation 'words, utterance, speech' would be better than 'voice'.

servuli . . . morientis: **morientis** is the present participle in the genitive agreeing with **servuli**. The diminutive is not used endearingly (as in Section 29), but rather to show contempt for Sassia by producing pathos for Strato: 'of the poor dying slave'.

36–37

In Sections 36 and 37, Cicero summarizes the charges he has made against Sassia and highlights her character as a wicked, evil woman with no morality. Notice the language he uses, creating an image of her not as a woman but as some beast, polluted and unwelcome to all, a beast whose sole focus is the destruction of her own son. It is rather an impressive indictment full of hyperbolic language and exclamations. It must have been an interesting performance to watch.

A Level

36

quod hoc portentum: Supply *est*: 'What monstrosity is this?' He refers, of course, to Sassia.

di immortales: Cicero is calling on the gods to help him explain Sassia's nature.

quod tantum monstrum in ullis locis: **quod** is used for balance with the **quod** at the beginning of the section and the **quod** in the next sentence. It is very difficult to fit it into the English, however. It is perhaps to translate it with **in ullis locis**: 'in what other places . . .'

aut unde natum esse dicamus: 'or where shall we say it was born?'

iam enim videtis profecto, iudices: Notice that Cicero invites the jury to reflect on all they have learnt and come to the same conclusion as he has.

non . . . dixisse: This is an indirect statement introduced by **videtis**. The subject of the indirect statement is **me** and the verb is **dixisse**: 'that I have spoken . . .'

non sine necessariis . . . ac maximis causis: **necessariis** and **maximis** are both adjectives agreeing with **causis** (this is an example of hendiadys). The use of **non sine** creates the effect of litotes: 'not without the greatest reasons of necessity'.

mali . . . sceleris: These words are partitive genitive after **nihil**: 'there is no evil, no wickedness . . .'

quod: Although **quod** is strictly singular, it refers to both **nihil mali** and **nihil sceleris**. It is singular because it refers to **nihil** both times.

illa: This refers to Sassia, of course.

ab initio: 'From the very beginning'. Cicero implies that Sassia has always hated her own son and has been plotting against him from the get-go.

voluerit, optaverit, cogitaverit, effecerit: These verbs build up to a crescendo; as we continue, the verbs have more active agency in bringing about the troubles for Cluentius.

nihil est . . . cogitatum: **cogitatum est** is the perfect passive of *cogito*: 'nothing has been planned . . .'

nihil . . . ab Oppianico sine consilio mulieris: There is a significant omission before this sentence in which Cicero brings up the attempted poisoning of Cluentius by Oppianicus the Elder. The Oppianicus referred to in this sentence is Oppianicus the Elder, which should be clear from the sentence which follows this one. Therefore the **nihil cogitatum** ('nothing planned') refers specifically in this context to the attempted poisoning of Cluentius. With this in mind, **consilio** is probably better translated as 'advice' or 'knowledge' since we cannot definitively say that Sassia planned the poisoning; Cicero is suggesting that she was aware of it.

quod nisi esset: **quod** is the connecting relative: 'if this had not been so . . .' **esset** is used rather than *fuisset* because Sassia is still alive at the time of the trial.

non . . . discessisset, sed . . . fugisset: Cicero is claiming that, if Sassia had not known about Oppianicus the Elder's attempt on her son's life, after it all came to light, 'she would not have left' as if from a wicked husband (**ut ab improbo viro**), 'but rather she would have fled' as if from the cruellest of enemies (**ut a crudelissimo hoste**). His point is that Sassia should have run away from Oppianicus the Elder if she had been any sort of mother to Cluentius.

in perpetuum: 'forever'.

scelere omni affluentem: 'that house overflowing with every sort of wickedness'.

nullum locum praetermisit: 'she passed by no place'. **locum** is more figurative here: 'she missed no opportunity'.

in quo non instrueret: The subjunctive is significant because it tells us that this is a purpose clause introduced by *qui* instead of *ut*. The **non** (although at first seeming out of place) is understood from the sense of the **nullum locum praetermisit**: 'she passed by no place in which she was not drawing up some plot . . .' i.e. every opportunity she had, she would draw up some plan against her son. 'she missed no opportunity to arrange some plot . . .'

ac dies omnes ac noctes: Notice that Cicero paints this as Sassia's obsession: she must find a way to ruin her son's life.

tota mente: Again, her obsession is worrying.

mater . . . filii: Once again, Cicero emphasizes the contrast between Sassia's relationship with Cluentius and her behaviour towards him.

cogitaret: This verb is subjunctive as it is still part of the purpose clause introduced by **in quo**: 'she missed no opportunity . . . to plan . . .'

quae: The connecting relative referring to Sassia: 'she'.

ut istum confirmaret Oppianicum accusatorem filio suo: A purpose clause explaining Sassia's actions in the main clause. **istum** is a demonstrative pronoun and makes it clear that we are talking about Oppianicus the Younger now (who is in the courtroom). **confirmaret** could be translated as 'give a backbone to', suggesting that Oppianicus the Younger is a weak figure who needed to be induced into being the prosecutor at this trial. **filio suo** is the dative of disadvantage: 'against her son'.

ut: This is a purpose clause: 'not only was she careful to prepare . . .'

cogitavit quibus . . . armaret: Notice that **armaret** is subjunctive and therefore **quibus** introduces a purpose clause: 'she also planned with what matters she might equip him (i.e. Oppianicus the Younger)'.

hinc . . . : The remainder of this paragraph is highly rhetorical and hyperbolic. Notice the use of repeated words or phrases (e.g. **hinc**, parts of *idem*, and parts of *accusator*) and the summary of her crimes, about which Cicero has already gone into detail.

hinc . . . hinc: 'From here'. **hinc** is effectively equivalent to 'for this reason' in this context. In both these clauses we must supply the verb *sunt*. Notice the parallelism: **hinc illae** . . .

sollicitationes: A *sollicitatio* is a 'vexation' which can be used to incite someone to do something. Our English word 'solicitation' derives from it. Perhaps it is best translated as 'inducements' here: 'those inducements of the slaves both by threats and promises'.

infinitae crudelissimaeque: Notice the two adjectives heightening the sense of disapproval of Sassia's judicial inquiry.

quaestiones: This is a specific reference to the torture of the slaves involved in Sassia's previous investigations.

quibus: A connecting relative in the dative (after **finem fecit**) referring to the **quaestiones**: 'made an end to these'.

non mulieris modus: It was not on account of any moderation on the part of Sassia; she did not have the morality to know that she had gone too far.

ab eodem scelere: 'from this same wickedness'.

triennio post: =*post triennium*: 'after three years'.

A Level

habitae: We must supply *sunt* to turn this into a perfect passive verb: 'those trials were held . . .'

eiusdem amentiae: 'of the same madness'. Cicero is using variatio, but the meaning is the same as *ab eadem amentia*.

falsae conscriptiones quaestionum: i.e. the forged documents mentioned in Section 35. We must supply the verb *sunt* (or even *scriptae sunt*).

ex eodem furore: 'from that same frenzy'. More variatio to keep the speech from getting stale. The use of this variatio also draws attention to the three nouns Cicero has used for Sassia's behaviour: *scelus*, *amentia* and *furor*. All these words carry extremely negative connotations.

conscelerata: This is an extremely strong adjective (made so by its compound formation): 'depraved'. Cutting out a man's tongue is a rather shocking thing to have done, and Cicero wants his jury to remember that.

totius . . . criminis: The word order of this clause is rather difficult, presumably to mirror just how involved in everything Sassia (**illa**) is. Translate as if it read *denique comparatio totius huius criminis* ('of this whole charge') *ab illa et inventa [est] et adornata est.*

denique: This is the culmination of Sassia's machinations: her son is now on trial for trumped up charges.

his rebus . . . instructum: **his rebus** is an ablative of instrument: 'fitted out with this ammunition'. **instructum** agrees with **accusatorem**.

accusatorem filio suo: Another repetition of this phrase to emphasize the peril of Cluentius' situation (he is being tried on a capital charge).

conquirendorum et conducendorum testium causa: **causa** and a gerund or gerundive (as here) can be used to express purpose. The gerundives agree with **testium** (for an explanation of gerundival attraction, see p. 50): 'for the sake of procuring and hiring witnesses'. Notice the use of the word **conducendorum** showing that Sassia had no honest witnesses and had to resort to paying them.

cum . . . ei nuntiatum est: Cicero is using the indicative **nuntiatum est** instead of the expected subjunctive to produce a vivid effect in the mind of the reader.

huius: A genitive case referring to Cluentius.

advolavit: A metaphorical use of the word, comparing Sassia to some sort of bird of prey and emphasizing her swiftness to see her son's misfortune (compare with its use in Section 4).

aut . . . deesset: Notice the chiasmus (dative, nominative, nominative, dative) drawing attention in particular to the second (more shocking) reason. *deesse* is followed by the dative and means 'to be lacking for [someone]': 'so that neither diligence was lacking for the prosecutors nor money for the witnesses'. We could turn the sentence round in English for a better flow: 'so that neither the prosecutors lacked diligence nor . . . etc'. Cicero again implies that all the witnesses have been bribed.

aut ne forte . . . amitteret: 'or perhaps so that she did not lose out on . . .'

mater hoc sibi optatissimum spectaculum: We are told that Sassia perhaps did not want to miss out on seeing 'this sight most wished for by her'. Notice the repetition of **mater** and its quite emphatic placement as well as the emphatic placement of **sibi optatissimum** between **hoc . . . spectaculum**. Of course, the use of the superlative is another fine touch in building up the character of Sassia.

huius sordium atque luctus et tanti squaloris: **huius** is genitive and refers to Cluentius: 'his'. **sordium, luctus** and **squaloris** are all genitives

A Level

after **spectaculum**: 'this sight of his mourning and grief and such unkempt clothing'. These words are not used metaphorically for Cluentius' current state, but rather literally: defendants in serious legal trials would often wear the unkempt clothes of a mourner to move the jury to pity.

37

quod iter: 'what journey'. This is the subject of the indirect statement introduced by **existimatis**: 'What journey do you think . . . ?'

quod ego . . . ex multis audivi et comperi: **quod** is a connecting relative and refers to 'the sort of journey' Sassia had to Rome. Cicero claims that he has heard and found out from many people what sort of journey she had.

propter vicinitatem Aquinatium et Fabraternorum: Aquinum and Fabrateria are towns in the south east of Latium. Cicero has got his information through means of the neighbourhood of the citizens of Aquinum and Fabrateria because these towns are close to Arpinum, where Cicero was born.

quos . . . esse factos: This is an indirect statement after **existimatis** from the first sentence of this section. **quod . . . comperi** was a small parenthesis explaining how Cicero came by his information; the grammar resumes from **quos**.

esse factos: The perfect infinitive of *fio*. We can just translate it as 'were' here.

mulierem quondam . . . possit: This whole phrase is an indirect statement. Although there is no verb introducing the indirect statement, it is implied that this is what people were saying to each other in their groans: 'To think that a woman . . .'

Larino: Ablative of origin: 'from Larinum'.

usque a mari supero: 'right from the *mare superum*'. The *mare superum* is the Adriatic.

quo facilius ... possit: **quo** is the usual introduction to a purpose clause which contains a comparative of some kind (e.g. **facilius**): 'To think that she is setting off to Rome so that she may be able more easily to ...' The use of the present subjunctive **possit** is dependent on the sense that this represents the direct words of the citizens; therefore it follows the primary sequence.

circumvenire: 'to surround'. Perhaps a less literal meaning of 'to cheat' would be a good translation here, since the charges brought against Cluentius are made up, according to Cicero.

iudicio capitis: **iudicio** is the ablative of instrument: 'with a capital charge'. For the use of **capitis** see the note on **periculum capitis** on p. 58.

filium: The use of this word again emphasizes the shock of the citizens as they discuss Sassia's motives for heading from Larinum to Rome.

nemo erat illorum: **illorum** is the partitive genitive after **nemo**: 'there was not one of them ...'

paene dicam: Cicero allows himself the concession that he cannot say that it was universally the case; however the rhetorical force of his sentence still stands even with this admission: 'I may say *almost* [no one]'

quin ... arbitraretur: **quin** stands for *qui ne* which is followed by a subjunctive. It is best translated as 'who ... not' in English: 'There was not one of them who did not think that ...'

expiandum: A gerundive of obligation (see p. 63) agreeing with **locum**. **arbitraretur** has introduced an indirect statement: 'think that that place needed to be purified'.

A Level

illum locum . . . quacunque: The **illum locum** is explained by the clause beginning **quacunque**: 'that place . . . wherever she . . .'

nemo quin: We must supply *erat illorum* as above: 'there was not one of them who . . . not'.

quae mater est omnium: This relative clause refers to **terram**. Cicero calls the earth the 'mother of all things' (a common description of the earth in ancient times) to allow him to sharpen the contrast with **consceleratae matris**. The ultimate mother (the earth) is being violated by the footsteps of this depraved mother (Sassia). Sassia's evil is so unmotherly that it is affecting Mother Earth.

consistendi potestas: 'the power of stopping'. **potestas** means 'opportunity' here.

ei fuit: The dative of possession: 'the opportunity was for her' = 'she had the opportunity'.

ex tot hospitibus: *hospites* may mean 'inn-keepers' rather than 'guest-friends'. Sassia finds that no one and nowhere will give her refuge.

qui non . . . fugeret: This is a generic subjunctive used in the relative clause giving a type of person; we can just translate it as a relative clause in English: 'not one was found who did not flee'.

contagionem aspectus: *fugio* takes a direct object in Latin. **contagionem aspectus** = 'the pollution of her glance'. **aspectus** is genitive singular.

se . . . committebat: 'she was entrusting herself'. The dative is used to show what Sassia is entrusting herself to.

ulli: This word is in the dative and qualifies both **urbi** and **hospiti**.

nunc vero: A strong start to the sentence bringing us back into the courtroom: 'But at this very moment'.

quid . . . quid . . . quid . . . : This tricolon of indirect questions is dependent on the main clause **quem ignorare nostrum putat**.

quem nostrum: nostrum is the partitive genitive from *nos*: 'which of us . . . ?' **quem nostrum** is the subject of the indirect statement introduced by **putat**.

quos . . . quibus . . . quorum: This is another tricolon of indirect questions, building to a crescendo accusing Sassia of bribery. These indirect questions are dependent on the verb **tenemus** which here is better translated as 'we know' (i.e. 'we have [in mind]').

quin: When used with the indicative (e.g. **cognovimus**), **quin** is simply an emphatic particle: 'indeed . . . !'

sacrificia . . . preces . . . vota cognovimus: cognovimus is technically a perfect tense but, with verbs of knowing, it can often be used for a present tense: 'we [have got to know in the past and therefore still] know'. Since **cognovimus** takes three direct objects here, it would be best to translate it as: 'we know about . . .'

quae putat occultiora esse: This relative clause refers to the **nocturna sacrificia. quae** is neuter accusative plural and is the subject of the indirect statement introduced by **putat. occultiora** is an 'absolute' comparative: 'which she thinks are so secret'.

nocturna . . . sceleratas . . . nefaria: Notice how the adjectives Cicero uses make even her religious observances sound dark and evil.

quibus: This is an ablative of instrument. This relative clause refers to all the nouns mentioned as the objects of **cognovimus**: i.e. **sacrificia**, **preces** and **vota**.

de suo scelere testatur: 'she calls [the immortal gods] as witnesses to her wickedness'. Sassia is polluting the gods themselves with her wickedness.

A Level

intellegit: This verb introduces an indirect statement. The subject of the indirect statement is **deorum mentes** and the verb is **posse** which has an accompanying infinitive **placari**: 'she does not understand that the minds of the gods are able to be appeased . . .'

non . . . superstitione neque . . . hostiis: *superstitio* implies some sort of excessive or unreasonable religious belief (rather than the proper *religio* which refers to the dutiful worship humans are bound to give to the gods). **hostiis** is from *hostia* (not *hostis*) and it means 'sacrificial victims'.

cuius: A connecting relative in the genitive and referring to Sassia: 'her'.

ego . . . confido: These words introduce an indirect statement: 'I believe that . . .' The subject of the indirect statement is **deos immortales** and the verb is **aspernatos esse**: 'that the immortal gods have rejected . . .'

furorem atque crudelitatem: Another example of hendiadys: 'raging cruelty'. This phrase is the object of **aspernatos esse**.

a suis aris atque templis: The suggestion that the gods have rejected Sassia from their places of worship is rather insulting. Cicero has painted Sassia as a woman who is completely unwelcome both to humans and gods; this hyperbolic portrayal is aimed at convincing the jury to despise Sassia and feel pity for her innocent son.

Vocabulary

An asterisk * denotes a word in OCR's Defined Vocabulary List for AS.

***a/ab/abs** +abl.	from, away from, by
abdo, abdere, abdidi, abditum	to hide, conceal
abhorreo, abhorrere, abhorrui	to shrink back from, shudder at
absolvo, absolvere, absolvi, absolutum	to set free, acquit
***absum, abesse, afui**	to be absent from, away from
***ac**	and
accedo, accedere, accessi, accessum	to come to, approach, arrive at
accusatio, accusationis f.	accusation, indictment, prosecution
accusator, accusatoris m.	prosecutor, plaintiff
accuso, accusare, accusavi, accusatum	to accuse, prosecute
acer, acris, acre	sharp, violent, keen
acerbe	harshly, bitterly, severely
acervatim	in a mass, summarily, briefly
***ad** +acc.	to, towards, at
adduco, adducere, adduci, adductum	to lead to, take to, bring to
***adeo**	so much, so greatly, to such an extent
adeo, adire, adii, aditum	to go towards, approach
adeo . . . potius	no . . . rather
aditus -us m.	approach, access, opportunity, attack
adiunctior, adiunctior, adiunctius	more closely connected
admiror, admirari, admiratus sum	to wonder at, be astonished at
adorno, adornare, adornavi, adornatum	to get ready, decorate
***adsum, adesse, adfui**	to be present, be here
***adulescens, adulescentis** c.	young person, youth
adulterinus -a -um	false, counterfeit, forged
aduncus -a -um	bent, hooked
advoco, advocare, advocavi, advocatum	to call, summon

advolo, advolare, advolavi, advolatum to fly at, run to, attack
aedes, aedis f. temple; [in pl.] house
aegroto, aegrotare, aegrotavi, aegrotatum to be ill, be sick
aetas, aetatis f. age, generation
affero, afferre, attuli, allatum to bring forward, convey
afficio, afficere, affeci, affectum to affect, bestow, punish
affinis, affinis m. relation by marriage
affluo, affluere, affluxi, affluxum to flow towards, overflow
age come on! come now!
***ager, agri** m. field, farm, territory
***aggredior, aggredi, aggressus sum** to approach, attack
***ago, agere, egi, actum** to do, act, drive
aio (2nd and 3rd person: **ais, ait, aiunt**) to say
aliquamdiu for a while, for any length of time
aliquando finally, at length, at last
aliquantum, aliquanti n. a considerable amount
***aliquis, aliquis, aliquid** someone, something, anyone, anything
***alius, alia, aliud** another, other
alligatus -a -um implicated, attached
alloquor, alloqui, allocutus sum to speak to, address
***alter, altera, alterum** one, another
amans, amantis loving
amens, amentis mad, mindless, out of one's mind
amentia -ae f. madness, senselessness, insanity, mindlessness
***amicus -i** m. friend
amita -ae f. (paternal) aunt
***amitto, amittere, amisi, amissum** to send away, lose
***amor, amoris** m. love, lust
***an** or
Anconitanus -i m. a person from Ancona
ango, angere, anxi, anctum to strangle, torment, trouble, vex
***animadverto, animadvertere, animadverti, animadversum** to notice, observe
***animus -i** m. spirit, soul, mind, courage
***annus -i** m. year

***ante** +acc.	before, in front of
ante	before
***antea**	before
aperte	openly, plainly
apertus -a -um	open, uncovered
appello, appellare, appellavi, appellatum	to call, address, speak to
***appropinquo, appropinquare, appropinquavi, appropinquatum** +dat.	to approach
***apud** +acc.	in, among, at, near, at the house of
Aquinas, Aquinatis	of Aquinum
***ara -ae** f.	altar
arbitror, arbitrari, arbitratus sum	to think, believe, decide
***arcesso, arcessere, arcessivi, arcessitum**	to summon, call forth
armarium -i n.	chest, wardrobe
armatus -i m.	armed man
armo, armare, armavi, armatum	to arm, equip
aspectus -us m.	sight, view, appearance
aspernor, aspernari, aspernatus sum	to disdain, reject, despise
aspicio, aspicere, aspexi, aspectum	to look at, look upon, behold
assiduus -a -um	continual, perpetual, incessant
***at**	but
***atque**	and
attamen	nevertheless
auctio, auctionis f.	auction, public sale
auctor, auctoris m.	guardian, trustee
auctoritas, auctoritatis f.	authority, influence
audacia -ae f.	boldness, audacity, impudence
***audax, audacis**	bold, daring, rash, audacious
***audeo, audere, ausus sum**	to dare
***audio, audire, audivi, auditum**	to hear, listen (to)
***aufero, auferre, abstuli, ablatum**	to take away, steal
***augeo, augere, auxi, auctum**	to increase, enlarge, strengthen
aurum -i n.	gold
auspex, auspicis c.	soothsayer
***aut . . . aut**	either . . . or
***autem**	but, however, moreover

aversor, aversari, aversatus sum to turn away, send away, reject, avoid
avia -ae f. grandmother

***bellum -i** n. war
benevolus -a -um well-wishing, kind, devoted
bestia -ae f. wild beast, animal
***brevis, brevis, breve** brief, short
breviter briefly, in short

***cado, cadere, cecidi, casum** to fall
***caedes, caedis** f. murder, slaughter, massacre
caedo, caedere, cecidi, caesum to kill, murder, slaughter
calamitas, calamitatis f. loss, harm, disaster
***capio, capere, cepi, captum** to catch, capture, take
***caput, capitis** n. head, life
***castra -orum** n. camp
casu by chance
***causa -ae** f. case, reason, trial, court-case, charge
***causa** +gen. for the sake of
celeriter quickly, fast
censorius -a -um of the censor, censorial
certe certainly, undoubtedly, assuredly
***ceteri -ae -a** other, remaining
circumforaneus -a -um travelling from market to market
circumseco, circumsecare to saw around
circumvenio, circumvenire, circumveni, circumventum to surround, cheat
***civitas, civitatis** f. citizenship, state, city, tribe
***clamo, clamare, clamavi, clamatum** to shout, call, cry
***clamor, clamoris** m. shout, call, uproar
***clarus -a -um** clear, famous, distinguished
coactor, coactoris m. money-collector
coarguo, coarguere, coargui to refute, prove guilty, convict of crime
***coepi, coepisse** to begin, have begun
***cogito, cogitare, cogitavi, cogitatum** to think, consider
cognatio, cognationis f. relationship, kin

cognatus -i m.	relation, kinsman
***cognosco, cognoscere, cognovi, cognitum**	to get to know, understand
***cogo, cogere, coegi, coactum**	to force, compel
colliquefactus -a -um	made liquid, completely dissolved
collocatio, collocationis f.	betrothal, giving in marriage
colonus -i m.	farmer
comburo, comburere, combussi, combustum	to burn up, cremate
comedo, comesse, comedi, comesum/ comestum	to eat up entirely, eat, consume
comitatus -us m.	escort, train, company
***committo, committere, commisi, commissum**	to entrust, act
commoror, commorari, commoratus sum	to stop, linger, stay
commoveor, commoveri, commotus sum	to be moved, be roused, be excited
communis, communis, commune	common, general, universal, public
comparatio, comparationis f.	preparation
compareo, comparere, comparui	to be evident, be plain, be present, appear
***comparo, comparare, comparavi, comparatum**	to prepare
comperio, comperire, comperi, compertum	to find out, ascertain, learn
comprobo, comprobare, comprobavi, comprobatum	to approve wholly, assent, agree
concordia -ae f.	harmony, union
concupio, concupere, concupivi, concupitum	to want very much, to long for
concursus -us m.	running together, concourse, assembly
***condemno, condemnare, condemnavi, condemnatum**	to sentence, condemn, convict
conditio, conditionis f.	agreement, condition, terms
conduco, conducere, conduxi, conductum	to assemble, collect, hire

conductum -i n.	a hired house
***confero, conferre, contuli, collatum**	to bring together, gather, collect
se conferre	to take oneself, go
confestim	immediately, without delay
***conficio, conficere, confeci, confectum**	to complete, accomplish, bring about
***confido, confidere, confisus sum**	to trust, believe
confirmo, confirmare, confirmavi, confirmatum	to make strong, strengthen, embolden
confiteor, confiteri, confessus sum	to acknowledge, admit, confess
conflo, conflare, conflavi, conflatum	to bring about, produce, cause
confugio, confugere, confugi	to flee to, take refuge with
confundo, confundere, confudi, confusum	to mix together, mingle, combine
congressio, congressionis f.	meeting, conference, association
conicio, conicere, conieci, coniectum	to throw forcibly, drive forcibly
coniungo, coniungere, coniunxi, coniunctum	to bind together, combine, form
***conor, conari, conatus sum**	to try, attempt
conquiro, conquirere, conquisivi, conquisitum	to collect, procure
consceleratus -a -um	wicked, depraved, villainous, criminal
conscientia -ae f.	knowledge, share, guilty knowledge
conscisco, consciscere, conscii, conscitum	to resolve upon, determine, decree
mortem sibi consciscere	to commit suicide
conscius -a -um	knowing, aware, conscious, an accomplice
conscribo, conscribere, conscripsi, conscriptum	to draw up, compose
conscriptio, conscriptionis f.	composition
consenesco, consenescere, consenui	to become weak, waste away, decay, fade
conservus -i m.	fellow-slave
***consilium -i** n.	council, plan, advice, prudence, wisdom

***consisto, consistere, constiti, constitum**	to halt, stand, stand firm
consobrinus -i m.	cousin
constantia -ae f.	firmness, constancy, consistency
***constituo, constituere, constitui, constitutum**	to decide, establish
***consul, consulis** m.	consul
consulto	deliberately, on purpose
contagio, contagionis f.	pollution, infection
contaminatus -a -um	polluted, impure, defiled
***contendo, contendere, contendi, contentum**	to strive for, pursue
contineo, continere, continui, contentum	to hold together, keep together, restrain, resolve
continuo	straightaway, directly, immediately
***contra** +acc.	against, opposite
contraho, contrahere, contraxi, contractum	to do business with, associate with
convalesco, convalescere, convalui	to recover, get better, grow strong
convivium -i n.	feast, banquet, dinner party
convoco, convocare, convocavi, convocatum	to call together, summon
copiose	in great abundance, copiously, fully
***corpus, corporis** n.	body, corpse
corrumpo, corrumpere, corrupi, corruptum	to bribe, corrupt
***crimen, criminis** n.	charge, accusation, crime
***crudelis, crudelis, crudele**	cruel
crudelitas, crudelitatis f.	harshness, cruelty, severity
crux, crucis f.	cross, execution
***cum**	when, since, although
***cum** +abl.	with, along with, together with
cupiditas, cupiditatis f.	desire, passion, lust
***cupidus -a -um**	desiring, desirous, eager, fond of
***cupio, cupere, cupivi, cupitum**	to desire, want, wish
***cur**	why
***curo, curare, curavi, curatum**	to care for, look after, see to, get done

damno, damnare, damnavi, damnatum	to condemn, judge guilty
***de** +abl.	down, down from, about, concerning
***debeo, debere, debui, debitum**	to owe, be bound; I ought, should, must
decem (indeclinable)	ten
decurio, decurionis m.	member of the municipal Senate, councillor
dedecus, dedecoris n.	disgrace, dishonour, infamy, shame
deduco, deducere, deduxi, deductum	to bring away, bring down
defensio, defensionis f.	defence, defence speech
defero, deferre, detuli, delatum	to bring down, report
nomen deferre	to indict, accuse, prosecute
***defessus -a -um**	exhausted, worn out, very tired
deicio, deicere, deieci, deiectum	to throw down
***deinde**	then, next, secondly
delatio, delationis f.	denunciation, accusation
delenio, delenire, delenivi, delenitum	to soothe, soften, charm, captivate
***deleo, delere, delevi, deletum**	to destroy
demonstro, demonstrare, demonstravi, demonstratum	to show, point out, indicate, represent
***denique**	finally, lastly, at last
dentatus -a -um	toothed, having teeth
denuntio, denuntiare, denuntiavi, denuntiatum	to denounce, threaten
deprehendo, deprehendere, deprehendi, deprehensum	to overtake, detect, find out
depromo, depromere, deprompsi, depromptum	to draw out, bring, fetch
desertus -a -um	deserted, abandoned
despondeo, despondere, despondi, desponsum	to promise, betroth, engage
desum, deesse, defui (+dat.)	to fail, be wanting, be lacking
detraho, detrahere, detraxi, detractum	to remove from, detract
***deus -i** m.	god
devincio, devincire, devinxi, devinctum	to bind up, oblige, enslave

***dico, dicere, dixi, dictum**	to say, speak, tell
***dies -ei** m. and f.	day
***difficilis, difficilis, difficile**	difficult
diffido, diffidere, diffisus sum	to distrust, have no faith in, despair of
digitus -i m.	finger
***dignitas, dignitatis** f.	merit, rank, dignity
***dignus -a -um**	worth of, deserving
***diligens, diligentis**	careful, diligent
diligentia -ae f.	carefulness, attentiveness, diligence
***dimitto, dimittere, dimisi, dimissum**	to send away, discharge, dismiss, postpone
***discedo, discedere, discessi, discessum**	to leave, depart
dissolutus -a -um	careless, negligent, inattentive
***diu**	for a long time
divortium -i n.	divorce
***do, dare, dedi, datum**	to give
***dolor, doloris** m.	pain, distress, grief
domesticus -a -um	domestic, household, private
***domina -ae** f.	mistress, lady
***dominus -i** m.	master
***domus -us** f.	house, home
***donum -i** n.	gift, present
***dormio, dormire, dormivi, dormitum**	to sleep, be asleep
***duco, ducere, duxi, ductum**	to lead, take, reckon
matrimonium ducere	to lead in marriage, marry
duo, duae, duo	two
***e(x)** +abl.	out of, from
ecce	look, behold, see
educo, educare, educavi, educatum	to bring up, rear, train
***efficio, efficere, effeci, effectum**	to carry out, accomplish
effrenatus -a -um	unbridled, unrestrained, unruly
***ego, mei**	I
egregius -a -um	extraordinary, distinguished, excellent

eicio, eicere, eieci, eiectum	to throw out, drive out, expel
eiusmodi	of that kind, of that sort
eloquens, eloquentis	eloquent, well-spoken
***emo, emere, emi, emptum**	to buy
emorior, emori, emortuus sum	to die off, die, perish
***enim**	for
epoto, epotare, epotavi, epotum	to drink up, drain, swallow
***equus -i** m.	horse
ergastulum -i n.	workhouse, penitentiary
eripio, eripere, eripui, ereptum	to snatch away, take away, steal
***erro, errare, erravi, erratum**	to wander, make a mistake
***et**	and
***et . . . et**	both . . . and
etenim	for indeed
***etiam**	also, even
***etsi**	although
exanimatus -a -um	lifeless, weakened, grief-stricken
***excito, excitare, excitavi, excitatum**	to rouse, wake up, stir up, incite
exclamo, exclamare, exclamavi, exclamatum	to call out, cry aloud, exclaim
excludo, excludere, exclusi, exclusum	to shut out, exclude, cut off
***exemplum -i** n.	example
exerceo, exercere, exercui, exercitum	to practise
exhaurio, exhaurire, exhausi, exhaustum	to drink up, empty, exhaust
existimatio, existimationis f.	reputation, character, honour
existimo, existimare, existimavi, existimatum	to value, estimate, reckon, think
exorior, exoriri, exortus sum	to come out, come forth, appear, spring up
experiens, experientis	experienced, enterprising, industrious
expio, expiare, expiavi, expiatum	to make amends, atone, make good
expono, exponere, exposui, expositum	to set forth, explain, relate
exseco, exsecere, exsecui, exsectum	to cut out, cut away
exsectio, exsectionis f.	cutting out, excision
exsequiae -arum f.	funeral procession, funeral
***exsilium -i** n.	exile, banishment

exsul, exsulis, c.	exile
exsulto, exsultare, exsultavi, exsultatum	to exult, rejoice exceedingly, revel, boast
***extra** +acc.	oustide
extremus -a -um	furthest, extreme, last
Fabraternus -a -um	belonging to Fabrateria
fabula -ae f.	tale, story, fable
facile	easily, quite
***facilis, facilis, facile**	easy
***facinus, facinoris** n.	crime, outrage, deed
***facio, facere, feci, factum**	to do, make
***fallo, fallere, fefelli, falsum**	to deceive, cheat, trick
falsus -a -um	deceptive, false, unfounded
***fama -ae** f.	reputation, talk, rumour, report, opinion
***familia -ae** f.	household, family
familiaris, familiaris m.	servant, friend, acquaintance
familiariter	intimately
fas (indeclinable) n.	that which is right, proper, lawful, permitted
febris, febris f.	fever
***fere**	nearly, about
***fero, ferre, tuli, latum**	to bring, bear, carry, relate
festus -a -um	of a festival, of a holiday, festive, festal
fictus -a -um	feigned, fictitious, false
***fidelis, fidelis, fidele**	faithful, loyal, trustworthy
***fides, ei** f.	faith, belief
***filia -ae** f.	daughter
***filius -i** m.	son
***finis, finis** m.	end, limit, death
***fio, fieri, factus sum**	to happen, become
firmo, firmare, firmavi, firmatum	to make firm, strengthen, fortify, support
firmus -a -um	strong, firm, powerful
flagro, flagrare, flagravi, flagratum	to burn, blaze, be inflamed, be stirred
fleo, flere, flevi, fletum	to weep, cry, lament

fletus -us m. — weeping
***forte** — by chance
***fortis, fortis, forte** — brave, strong
***fortuna -ae** f. — fortune, fate, chance, luck
***forum -i** n. — forum, market-place
***frater, fratris** m. — brother
fraternus -a -um — of a brother, brotherly
fruor, frui, fructus sum (+abl.) — to enjoy, delight in
***fuga -ae** f. — flight, fleeing, escape
***fugio, fugere, fugi, fugitum** — to flee, run away from
fundamentum -i n. — foundation, basis
fundus -a -um — bottom
funestus -a -um — deady, fatal, calamitous, dismal
funus, funeris n. — funeral procession, burial, funeral
furo, furere, furui — to rage, rave, be mad
***furor, furoris** m. — raving, rage, madness, fury
furtum -i n. — theft, robbery

Gallicanus -i m. — a Gaul
Gallicus -a -um — Gallic, of Gaul
***gaudium -i** n. — joy, gladness, delight
gemitus -us m. — sigh, groan, lamentation
gener, generi m. — son-in-law
grandis, grandis, grande — full-grown, large, great, grand
gravidus -a -um — laden, pregnant, with child
graviter — gravely, seriously, heavily
gremium -i n. — lap

***habeo, habere, habui, habitum** — to have, hold, reckon
hereditas, hereditatis f. — inheritance
heres, heredis c. — heir
***hic, haec, hoc** — this
***hic** — here
hicce, haecce, hocce — emphatic form of **hic, haec hoc**
***hinc** — from here, hence
***homo, hominis** c. — man, person, human being
honestus -a -um — honourable, distinguished, respectable, honoured

***honor, honoris** m.	public office, position of honour, honour
***hora -ae** f.	hour
***hospes, hospitis** m.	host, guest, friend
hostia -ae f.	sacrificial victim, sacrifice
hostilis, hostilis, hostile	hostile, of an enemy
***hostis, hostis** c.	enemy
***huc**	to this place, to here, hither
humanitas, humanitatis f.	humanity, gentleness, kindness
iactura -ae f.	loss, cost
***iam**	now, already
***ibi**	there
idcirco	for that reason, on that account
***idem, eadem, idem**	the same
***igitur**	therefore
ignarus -a -um	ignorant, unaware, not knowing
***ignoro, ignorare, ignoravi, ignoratum**	to be ignorant, not know, have no knowledge of
***ille, illa, illud**	that
***illic**	there
immanis, immanis, immane	monstrous, enormous, huge
immortalis, immortalis, immortale	immortal, deathless
***impero, imperare, imperavi, imperatum** (+dat.)	to order, command
impius -a -um	without respect, wicked
importunitas, importunitatis f.	incivility, rudeness, insolence
importunus -a -um	troublesome, shameless, cruel, uncivil
improbitas, improbitatis f.	wickedness, depravity, impudence
improbus -a -um	dishonest, bad, wicked
impudens, impudentis	shameless, without shame, impudent
impudentia -ae f.	shamelessness
***in** +abl.	in, on, among
***in** +acc.	into, onto, to, against
inauditus -a -um	unheard of, strange
incertus -a -um	uncertain, doubtful, untrustworthy
incido, incidere, incidi	to fall into, fall in with

incolumis, incolumis, incolume unharmed, uninjured, safe, unimpaired
incredibilis, incredibilis, incredibile unbelievable, beyond belief, unparalleled
index, indicis c. informer, guide
indicium -i n. sign, indication, proof
indico, indicare, indicavi, indicatum to point out, show, disclose, reveal
indigne unworthily, undeservedly, shamefully
indomitus -a -um untameable, ungovernable, fierce, wild
ineptiae -arum f. sillinesses, fooleries, absurdities
inermis, inermis, inerme unarmed, defenceless
infans, infantis c. baby, infant, child
inferus -a -um below
infestus -a -um hostile, dangerous, troublesome
infinitus -a -um boundless, unlimited, endless
infirmus -a -um weak, feeble
inimicitia -ae f. enmity, hostility
*__inimicus -i__ m. enemy
*__initium -i__ n. beginning, start
*__iniuria -ae__ f. injustice, wrong, injury
innocens, innocentis harmless, guiltless, innocent
*__inquam__ (3rd person: **inquit, inquiunt**) to say, speak
insequor, insequi, insecutus sum to pursue, censure, reproach
*__insidiae -arum__ f. trap, ambush
insimulo, insimulare, insimulavi, insimulatum to charge, accuse
instituo, instituere, institui, institutum to begin, appoint
*__instruo, instruere, instruxi, instructum__ to draw up, furnish, fit out
integer, integra, integrum complete, whole
de integro again, fresh
*__intellego, intellegere, intellexi, intellectum__ to understand, perceive, get to know
*__inter__ +acc. among, between
intercedo, intercedere, intercessi, intercessum to come between, pass

***interea**	meanwhile
***interficio, interficere, interfeci, interfectum**	to kill
***interim**	meanwhile
interitus -us m.	death, destruction, ruin
intervallum -i n.	interval, intermission, respite
***intra** +acc.	inside, within
introduco, introducere, introduxi, introductum	to lead in, bring in
intueor, intueri, intuitus sum	to look upon, look at
inultus -a -um	unpunished, with impunity
inusitatus -a -um	unusual, uncommon, extraordinary
***invenio, invenire, inveni, inventum**	to find, find out
investigo, investigare, investigavi, investigatum	to track, search for, look into, investigate
invideo, invidere, invidi, invisum (+dat.)	to begrudge, envy
***invitus -a -um**	unwilling, reluctant
***ipse, ipsa, ipsum**	himself, herself, itself
***is, ea, id**	this, that; he, she, it
iste, ista, istud	this, that
***ita**	in such a way, thus, so, to such an extent
Italicus -a -um	Italian
***itaque**	therefore, and so
***iter, itineris** n.	journey
***iterum**	again
***iubeo, iubere, iussi, iussum**	to order, command
iucundus -a -um	pleasant, agreeable, pleasing, delightful
***iudex, iudicis** m.	judge, juryman
iudicium -i n.	judgement, trial, sentence
iudico, iudicare, iudicavi, iudicatum	to judge, be a judge, pass judgement, decide
iuro, iurare, iuravi, iuratum	to swear (an oath)
iuste	legitimately, by law, justly
***iustus -a -um**	just, upright, righteous

labefacto, labefactare, labefactavi, labefactatum	to shake, weaken, overthrow, destroy
lacrima -ae f.	tear
***laedo, laedere, laesi, laesum**	to hurt, wound, injure, damage, trouble
laetitia -ae f.	joy, happiness, rejoicing
laetor, laetari, laetatus sum	to rejoice, feel joy, be glad
Larinas, Larinatis	of Larinum
late	broadly, widely, extensively
***latus, lateris** n.	side, flank
legatum -i n.	bequest, legacy
lego, legare, legavi, legatum	to leave a legacy, bequeath
***lex, legis** f.	law, principle, rule
libenter	gladly
***liberi -orum** c.	children
libido, libidinis f.	desire, passion, lust
lingua -ae f.	tongue
***litterae -arum** f.	letter, letters
litura -ae f.	erasure, blotting out, correction
***locus -i** m.	place, location
***longus -a -um**	long
loquax, loquacis	talkative, chatty, loquacious
***loquor, loqui, locutus sum**	to speak, say
luceo, lucere, luxi	to be light, to shine
luctus -us m.	sorrow, mourning, grief
ludi -orum m.	the games
ludus -i m.	game, school
macula -ae f.	stain, fault, blot, disgrace
maereo, maerere	to be sad, mourn, grieve, lament
maeror, maeroris m.	mourning, sadness, sorrow, grief
***magnus -a -um**	big, great, large
maleficium -i n.	evil deed, offence, crime, injury
***malo, malle, malui**	to prefer, choose rather
***malus -a -um**	bad, evil
***maneo, manere, mansi, mansum**	to remain, stay, endure
manifesto	clearly, openly, evidently
***manus -us** f.	hand; band of men
***mare, maris** n.	sea

***mater, matris** f.	mother
matrimonium -i n.	marriage
maturo, maturare, muturavi, maturatum	to hasten, accelerate
maximus -a -um	greatest, biggest
medicina -ae f.	medicine
medicus -i m.	doctor
mediocris, mediocris, mediocre	medium, moderate
***medius -a -um**	middle
memoria -ae f.	memory, remembrance
mendax, mendacis	deceitful, mendacious, a liar
***mens, mentis** f.	mind
mentior, mentiri, mentitus sum	to lie, deceive, cheat
metuo, metuere, metui, metutum	to fear, be afraid
***metus -us** m.	fear, dread
***meus -a -um**	my
milia -ium n.	thousands [pl. of **mille**]
mille (indeclinable) n.	a thousand
***mille passus, mille passuum** n.	mile (a thousand paces)
minae, arum f.	threats
minime	very little, by no means
minor, minoris	less, younger
minutus -a -um	small, insignificant, unimportant
***miror, mirari, miratus sum**	to wonder (at), be amazed (by)
mirus -a -um	wonderful, extraordinary, astonishing
***miser, misera, miserum**	wretched, sad, miserable
misericordia -ae f.	pity, sympathy, compassion
***mitto, mittere, misi, missum**	to send
***modo**	only, just
***modus -i** m.	way, manner, kind
molestia -ae f.	trouble, annoyance, distress
molior, moliri, molitus sum	to set oneself to, labour upon, work, attempt
monstrum -i n.	monster
***mora -ae** f.	delay
***morbus -i** m.	illness, disease
***morior, mori, mortuus sum**	to die
***mors, mortis** f.	death

muliebris, muliebris, muliebre — of a woman, womanly, feminine
***mulier, mulieris** f. — woman, wife
multo, multare, multavi, multatum — to punish
***multus -a -um** — much, a lot
municeps, municipis c. — townsperson
municipium -i n. — town, township
***munio, munire, munivi, munitum** — to fortify, defend, protect, build the way
***munus, muneris** n. — duty, service, gift
***muto, mutare, mutavi, mutatum** — to change, alter

***nam** — for
***nascor, nasci, natus sum** — to be born
***natura -ae** f. — nature
***ne** +subj. — in order that . . . not, so that . . . not, that . . . not, lest
***-ne** — (introduces a question)
***ne . . . quidem** — not even
***nec** — and . . . not
necessarius -i m. — relation, relative, friend, companion
***neco, necare, necavi, necatum** — to kill
nefarius -a -um — impious, abominable, nefarious
***negotium -i** n. — business, affair
***nemo, nullius** c. — nobody, not one
nepos, nepotis m. — grandson
nequaquam — in no way, by no means
neque — and not
neque . . . neque — neither . . . nor
***nescio, nescire, nescivi, nescitum** — not to know
***nihil** (indeclinable) n. — nothing
nimium — too much
***nisi** — if . . . not, unless, except
***nobilis, nobilis, nobile** — high born, renowned
nobilitas, nobilitatis f. — high birth, nobility, excellence
nocens, nocentis — wicked, bad, criminal, harmful, guilty
***noceo, nocere, nocui, nocitum** (+dat.) — to do harm, hurt
***noctu** — at night, by night

nocturnus -a -um	nocturnal, of night
***nolo, nolle, nolui**	to be unwilling, not want
***nomen, nominis** n.	name, clan, reputation
nomino, nominare, nominavi, nominatum	to name
***non**	not
***nondum**	not yet
***nonne**	surely . . . ? [expects the answer yes]
***nos, nostrum/nostri**	we
***noster, nostra, nostrum**	our
***novus -a -um**	new, novel, strange
***nox, noctis** f.	night
nubilis, nubilis, nubile	marriageable, of marriageable age
nubo, nubere, nupsi, nuptum (+dat.)	to marry (of a woman)
***nullus -a -um**	not any, none, no
nummus -i m.	coin, money
***numquam**	never
***nunc**	now
***nuntio, nuntiare, nuntiavi, nuntiatum**	to announce
nuper	recently
nuptiae -arum f.	marriage
o	oh
obscurus -a -um	obscure, dark, hidden, secret
obsignator, obsignatoris m.	sealer, witness
obsigno, obsignare, obsignavi, obsignatum	to sign and seal (as a witness)
obstringo, obstringere, obstrinxi, obstrictum	to bind, oblige, lay under obligation
occido, occidere, occidi, occasum	to die, perish
***occido, occidere, occidi, occisum**	to strike down, kill
occultus -a -um	hidden, secret, concealed
***odi, odisse**	to hate
***odium -i** n.	hatred
offendo, offendere, offendi, offensum	to hit, come upon, meet with, find
offensus -a -um	offensive, hateful
***offero, offerre, obtuli, oblatum**	to present, offer

omen, ominis n.	omen, sign, token
***omnis, omnis, omne**	all, every, entire, whole
***oppidum -i** n.	town
***opprimo, opprimere, oppressi, oppressum**	to overcome, defeat
oppugnatio, oppugnationis f.	attack, assault
***oppugno, oppugnare, oppugnavi, oppugnatum**	to attack
optatus -a -um	wished for, longed for, desired
optimus -a -um	best, very good, excellent
opto, optare, optavi, optatum	to wish, desire, choose
***opus, operis** n.	work, labour, toil
***oratio, orationis** f.	speech, oration
***orior, oriri, ortus sum**	to rise, start, originate
ornatus -a -um	excellent, distinguished, eminent
ostento, ostentare, ostentavi, ostentatum	to show, offer, hold out, threaten
***paene**	almost, nearly
***palam**	openly
panis, panis m.	bread, food
paries, parietis m.	wall, partition-wall
parricidium -i n.	murder of a close relation
***pars, partis** f.	part, share
partior, partiri, partitus sum	to divide, apportion, share
partus -us m.	birth, delivery
***parvus -a -um**	small, little, paltry
patefacio, patefacere, patefeci, patefactum	to lay open, throw open, disclose
***pater, patris** m.	father
***patior, pati, passus sum**	to suffer, endure, allow
***pauci -ae -a**	(a) few, little
***paullisper**	for a little while, for a short time
***pecunia -ae** f.	money
pelicatus -us m.	concubinage, rivalry
pellicio, pellicere, pellexi, pellectum	to allure, entice, coax, win over
penitus	deeply
***per** +acc.	through, along
percuriosus -a -um	very curious, highly inquisitive

perditus -a -um	hopeless, deserate, ruined, corrupt
***perdo, perdere, perdidi, perditum**	to lose, destroy, ruin
***pereo, perire, perii, peritum**	to perish, die
perfero, perferre, pertuli, perlatum	to bear through, suffer, endure
***perficio, perficere, perfeci, perfectum**	to carry out, bring to pass
perfringo, perfringere, perfregi, perfractum	to break through, break to pieces, violate
perfugium -i n.	shelter, asylum, refuge
***periculum -i** n.	danger
permano, permanare, permanavi, permanatum	to flow through, spread through, penetrate
pernicies -ei f.	destruction, death, ruin
perniciosus -a -um	destructive, ruinous, baleful
perpetuus -a -um	continuous, everlasting, perpetual
perquiro, perquirere, perquisivi, perquisitum	to make inquiry, inquire diligently
perspicio, perspicere, perspexi, perspectum	to look closely at, inspect, see clearly
***persuadeo, persuadere, persuasi, persuasum** (+dat.)	to persuade, convince
pertimeo, pertimere, pertimui	to fear very greatly, be very afraid
pertineo, pertinere, pertinui	to reach, relate to, pertain to
***pervenio, pervenire, perveni, perventum**	to come through, come to, arrive at
pestis, pestis f.	deadly disease, plague, pestilence, pest
***peto, petere, petivi, petitum**	to seek, beseech, make for, attack
pharmacopola -ae m.	drug-seller
pie	dutifully, according to duty
pietas, pietatis f.	duty, sense of duty (to the gods, country and family)
piscina -ae f.	pond
placo, placare, placavi, placatum	to please, appease, pacify
***plenus -a -um** (+gen.)	full (of), mature
plus, pluris n.	more
poculum -i n.	cup, drinking-vessel
***poena -ae** f.	punishment, penalty
Poenae -arum f.	Deities of Vengeance

pondo	in weight, by weight
***populus -i** m.	people
***porta -ae** f.	gate
portentum -i n.	monster, monstrosity
***possum, posse, potui**	to be able
***post** +acc.	after
***postea**	after, afterwards
posteaquam	afterwards
***postquam**	after, afterwards, when
***postremo**	lastly, finally
***postridie**	on the next day
***postulo, postulare, postulavi, postulatum**	to demand, ask for
***potestas, potestatis** f.	power, authority, opportunity, ability
potio, potionis f.	drink, draught
potissimum	chiefly, principally, especially
***potius**	rather
praeceps, praecipitis	headlong
praeclarus -a -um	magnificent, remarkable, splendid, excellent
praeditus -a -um	endowed with, possessed of
praeiudico, praeiudicare, praeiudicavi, praeiudicatum	to judge beforehand
praesens, praesentis	present, in person, face to face
***praeter** +acc.	except
***praeterea**	moreover, besides
praetereo, praeterire, praeterii, praeteritum	to pass over, omit, leave out, not mention
praetermitto, praetermittere, praetermisi, praetermissum	to pass by, omit, neglect
prehendo, prehendere, prehendi, prehensum	to lay hold of, grasp, seize
***pretium -i** n.	price, value
prex, precis f.	prayer
primo	at first, firstly
primum	firstly
***primus -a -um**	first, chief, best
***princeps, principis** c.	first, chief, leader

principium -i n.	beginning, commencement, outset
***prius**	before
***pro** +acc.	on account of, because of, before
probabilis, probabilis, probabile	likely, credible, probable
***procedo, procedere, processi, processum**	to advance, proceed
profecto	actually, indeed, assuredly
profero, proferre, protuli, prolatum	to bring forth, produce
***proficiscor, proficisci, profectus sum**	to set out
profugio, profugere, profugi	to flee from, escape from
***promitto, promittere, promisi, promissum**	to promise
propero, properare, properavi, properatum	to hurry, hasten, be quick
propinquus -i m.	relation, relative
propior, propior, propius	nearer, closer
propono, proponere, proposui, propositum	to put forth, set out, propose
***propter** +acc.	on account of
proscribo, proscribere, proscripsi, proscriptum	to outlaw, proscribe
proscriptio, proscriptionis f.	proscription
prosterno, prosternere, prostravi, prostratum	to scatter in front, throw down, overthrow
***publicus -a -um**	public, common, of the state
pudicitia -ae f.	modesty, chastity, virtue
***pudor, pudoris** m.	shame, sense of shame, modesty, decency
***puer, pueri** m.	boy
punctum -i n.	dot, moment, instant
***puto, putare, putavi, putatum**	to think
***quaero, quaerere, quaesivi, quaesitum**	to seek, ask, gain
quaeso	I beg, pray, beseech, entreat
quaestio, quaestionis f.	inquiry, investigation, court
***quam**	than
***quam** + superlative	as . . . as possible
***quam**	how!

quamobrem	why? on account of what?
***quantus -a -um**	how much? how great?
***quasi**	as if, just as, nearly
quattuorviri -orum m.	council of four
***-que**	and
quemadmodum	just as, how
querimonia -ae f.	complaint, lament
***queror, queri, questus sum**	to complain, lament
***qui, quae, quod**	which
quicunque, quaecunque, quodcunque	whoever, whatever
quid?	what about this? why? consider the following
***quidam, quaedam, quoddam**	a, a certain, someone
***quidem**	indeed
quiesco, quiescere, quievi, quietum	to keep quiet, rest, desist
quin +subj.	who ... not
quin +indic.	indeed, moreover
quinque (indeclinable)	five
***quis, quis, quid**	who? what?
quisnam, quaenam, quidnam	who on earth? what on earth?
***quisquam, quisquam, quicquam**	anyone, anything
***quisquis, quisquis, quicquid/quidquid**	whoever, whatever
***quod**	because
quotidianus -a -um	daily
quotidie	everyday, daily
***ratio, rationis** f.	reckoning, reasoning, reason, understanding, judgement
***recipio, recipere, recepi, receptum**	to regain, receive, welcome
***recito, recitare, recitavi, recitatum**	to read aloud, recite
recordor, recordari, recordatus sum	to remember, recollect
recupero, recuperare, recuperavi, recuperatum	to recover, regain
recuso, recusare, recusavi, recusatum	to refuse
***reddo, reddere, reddidi, redditum**	to give back, return, restore
redundo, redundare, redundavi, redundatum	to overflow, be soaked with

reformido, reformidare, reformidavi, reformidatum	to fear greatly, dread, shun
regio, regionis f.	region, district, neighbourhood
religio, religionis f.	worship, rites
***relinquo, relinquere, reliqui, relictum**	to leave, leave behind, abandon
***reliquus -a -um**	left, remaining
remedium -i n.	cure, remedy, medicine
remotus -a -um	removed, distant, separate
renuntio, renuntiare, renuntiavi, renuntiatum	to announce, report
***repente**	suddenly, unexpectedly
repentinus -a -um	sudden, unexpected
reperio, reperire, repperi, repertum	to find out, discover, learn
***res -ei** f.	thing, affair, matter, business
***respondeo, respondere, respondi, responsum**	to reply
restituo, restituere, restitui, restitutum	to rebuild, restore, give back
resto, restare, restiti	to be left, remain
reus -i m.	defendant
revertor, reverti	to turn back, come back, return
revoco, revocare, revocavi, revocatum	to call back, recall, draw back
rumor, rumoris m.	talk, hearsay, rumour
sacrificium -i n.	sacrifice
***saepe**	often
salvus -a -um	safe, uninjured, unharmed
***sanguis, sanguinis** m.	blood
***satis**	enough, sufficient, satisfactory
satisfacio, satisfacere, satisfeci, satisfactum	to satisfy, content, make amends, pay a debt
sceleratus -a -um	wicked, bad, impious
***scelus, sceleris** n.	crime, wickedness, sin
***scio, scire, scivi, scitum**	to know
***scribo, scribere, scripsi, scriptum**	to write, appoint
***se, sui**	himself, herself, itself, themselves
secerno, secernere, secrevi, secretum	to separate, part, distinguish
***sed**	but

***sedes, sedis** f.	seat, home, abode
***senator, senatoris** m.	senator
sensus -us m.	feeling, sense, perception, sensation
***sententia -ae** f.	opinion, judgement, sentence
***sentio, sentire, sensi, sensum**	to feel, notice, sense, perceive
sepelio, sepelire, sepilivi, sepultum	to bury
sequester, sequestris m.	depositary, trustee, agent
sermo, sermonis m.	conversation, discourse, speech
sero	too late
serrula -ae f.	small saw
servitus, servitutis f.	slavery, servitude
***servo, servare, servavi, servatum**	to save, protect, keep
servulus -i m.	slave-boy
***servus -i** m.	slave
***si**	if
***sic**	thus, in this way
sicarius -i m.	cutthroat, assassin
sicuti	just as, as
significatio, significationis f.	expression, indication
***signum -i** n.	sign, mark, token, signature
***similis, similis, simile**	like, similar
***simul**	at the same time, together
simulo, simulare, simulavi, simulatum	to pretend
simultas, simultatis f.	hostile encounter, enmity, grudge, hatred
sin	but if
***sine** +abl.	without
singularis, singularis, singulare	unique, extraordinary, unparalleled
***sino, sinere, sivi, situm**	to allow, permit, suffer
sinus -us m.	fold, bosom, breast, lap
socrus -us f.	mother-in-law
solatium -i n.	comfort, relief, consolation, solace
***soleo, solere, solitus sum**	to be accustomed to
solitudo, solitudinis f.	loneliness, solitude
sollicitatio, sollicitationis f.	vexation, anxiety, instigation
sollicitudo, sollicitudinis f.	uneasiness, anxiety, worry

***solum**	only, just
sordes, sordis f.	dirt, mourning
***soror, sororis** f.	sister
spectaculum -i n.	sight, spectacle, show
***spero, sperare, speravi, speratum**	to hope, expect
***spes, -ei** f.	hope
squalor, squaloris m.	dirtiness, filthy garments, mourning garments
***statim**	immediately, at once
strictim	briefly, cursorily, summarily
struo, struere, struxi, structum	to devise, contrive
***stultus -a -um**	stupid, foolish
***subito**	suddenly
subitus -a -um	sudden
***sum, esse, fui**	to be
summatim	briefly, shortly, summarily
***summus -a -um**	uppermost, highest, top (of), height of
superior, superioris	higher, former, previous
superstitio, superstitionis f.	superstition
***superus -a -um**	upper, higher
supplicium -i n.	punishment, death penalty, death
***suscipio, suscipere, suscepi, susceptum**	to take up, undertake, acknowledge a child
suspicio, suspicionis f.	mistrust, distrust, suspicion
suspiciosus -a -um	suspicious, suspected
***suspicor, suspicari, suspicatus sum**	to suspect, mistrust
***suus -a -um**	his, her, its, their
***taberna -ae** f.	shop, inn
tabula -ae f.	writing-tablet, account book, record
***tam**	so
tamdiu	for so long
***tamen**	however
tametsi	although
***tandem**	finally, at last, at length
***tantus -a -um**	so great, so big

***tectum** -i n.	roof, building, house
***templum** -i n.	temple
***tempus, temporis** n.	time, season, occasion
***teneo, tenere, tenui, tentum**	to hold, keep, maintain
tento, tentare, tentavi, tentatum	to try, test
***terra -ae** f.	land, ground, earth
***terreo, terrere, terrui, territum**	to frighten, terrify
tertius -a -um	third
testamentum -i n.	will
testimonium -i n.	evidence, testimony
testis, testis c.	witness
testor, testari, testatus sum	to declare, call to witness
***timeo, timere, timui**	to fear, be afraid
***timor, timoris** m.	fear
***tollo, tollere, sustuli, sublatum**	to take up, raise, remove, destroy, kill
tormentum -i n.	instrument of torture, torture
tortor, tortoris m.	torturer
tortuosus -a -um	full of crooks, twisted
***tot**	so many
***totus -a -um**	whole, complete
transcribo, transcribere, transcripsi, transcriptum	to transfer, copy out
transigo, transigere, transegi, transactum	to come to an agreement, do a deal
tres, tres, tria	three
triennium -i n.	period of three years
triumpho, triumphare, triumphavi, triumphatum	to celebrate a triumph, go in triumph
***tu, tui**	you
***tum**	then, at that time
tutor, tutoris m.	guardian, protector
***tuus -a -um**	your
***ullus -a -um**	any, any one
***umquam**	ever
***una**	together with
***unde**	from where, whence
undecimus -a -um	eleventh

***undique**	from all sides, on all sides
universus -a -um	whole, entire, all, every
unus, una, unum	one
unusquisque, unaquaeque, unumquidque	each single one
***urbs, urbis** f.	city
***usque**	all the way, right up to, continuously
***ut** +indic.	as, when, how
***ut** +subj.	in order that, so that, that
***uterque, utraque, utrumque**	each (of two), both
***utor, uti, usus sum** (+abl.)	to use, be intimate with
***utrum**	whether
***uxor, uxoris** f.	wife
vagus -a -um	wandering, travelling
***valeo, valere, valui, valitum**	to be strong, be healthy, be well
valetudo, valetudinis f.	state of health, health
vehemens, vehementis	violent, furious
***vehementer**	violently, loudly, strongly
vena -ae f.	vein
venenum -i n.	poison
veneo, venire, venivi, venitum	to be sold, be on sale
***venio, venire, veni, ventum**	to come, go
***verbum -i** n.	word
***vereor, vereri, veritus sum**	to fear, be afraid
veritas, veritatis f.	truth
***vero**	indeed
versor, versari, versatus sum	to dwell, be situated, be concerned
verum	but, certainly
***verus -a -um**	true
***vester, vestra, vestrum**	your
vestigium -i n.	footprint, trace, clue
vestigo, vestigare, vestigavi, vestigatum	to track, discover, inquire into, investigate
vicinitas, vicinitatis f.	vicinity, neighbourhood
***victor, victoris** m.	victor, winner, conqueror
***victoria -ae** f.	victory
victrix, victricis f.	victor, conqueror

***video, videre, vidi, visum**	to see
***videor, videri, visus sum**	to seem, appear
***vinco, vincere, vici, victum**	to conquer, win, defeat
vinculum -i n.	chain, fetter
violo, violare, violavi, violatum	to dishonour, injure, defile
***vir, viri** m.	man, husband
***virtus, virtutis** f.	virtue, courage, excellence
***vis** (irreg.) f.	force, violence, punishment
***vita -ae** f.	life, lifetime
vitricus -i m.	step-father
***vivo, vivere, vixi, victum**	to live, be alive
***vivus -a -um**	alive, living
***vix**	scarcely, with difficulty
vociferatio, vociferationis f.	loud calling, clamour, cry
***volo, velle, volui**	to want, be willing
voluntas, voluntatis f.	desire, wish, intention, disposition
***vos, vestrum/vestri**	you (pl.)
votum -i n.	vow, promise
***vox, vocis** f.	voice
***vultus -us** m.	face, expression